To Tracy

With love and
peace
Lisa

My Spiritual Inheritance Devotional

Juanita Bynum

Charisma
HOUSE
A STRANG COMPANY

Most STRANG COMMUNICATIONS/CHARISMA HOUSE/SILOAM products are available at special quantity discounts for bulk purchase for sales promotions, premiums, fund-raising, and educational needs. For details, write Strang Communications/Charisma House/ Siloam, 600 Rinehart Road, Lake Mary, Florida 32746, or telephone (407) 333-0600.

MY SPIRITUAL INHERITANCE DEVOTIONAL by Juanita Bynum
Published by Charisma House
A Strang Company
600 Rinehart Road
Lake Mary, Florida 32746
www.charismahouse.com

Cover design by Judith McKittrick
Interior design by Terry Clifton

Library of Congress Cataloging-in-Publication Data
Bynum, Juanita.
My spiritual inheritance devotional / Juanita Bynum.
    p. cm.
ISBN 1-59185-559-4 (hardback)
1. Spiritual formation. 2. Meditations. I. Title.
BV4511.B97 2004
242--dc22

                            2004011112
                    05 06 07 08 09— 987654321
                Printed in the United States of America

Contents

Introduction

*E*verywhere I go, I see the onset of a mighty revival across this nation. People everywhere are being embraced and ushered into the body of Christ. People across the country are learning what it means to have their old heart removed and replaced with a new heart, a heart that beats for God and longs to walk in His ways.

But you see, it is possible to have the experience of salvation and even receive a new heart, but still miss the experience of walking into your spiritual destiny—your spiritual inheritance—which is to be planted into your new heart.

God is concerned that this not happen to you! He longs for you to not only receive a new heart, but also that you come into the full portion of your spiritual inheritance—the destiny that is waiting for you in Him, your fullest potential.

His portion will change you. It will birth you into destiny. When you are receiving your spiritual portion from God, it will feed your spirit. As your spirit grows, you will come to maturity in Christ. And as Christians everywhere mature in Christ, maturity comes to the body of Christ. So we must be sure we are really getting the Father's portion.

This one-hundred-day devotional journey will help you to discover how to receive your spiritual inheritance. You will discover, as I discovered, that God has placed in our lives men and women of God who function as spiritual fathers and mothers to us. Your spiritual inheritance is linked to spiritual investment that you must allow your spiritual father or mother to make into your life. Through the counsel and wisdom of your spiritual parents will come the impartation of divine destiny. To receive from the Father, you must first be able to acknowledge that God can give your leader the ability to see into your life and to tap into the Spirit. If you learn to do this, the Spirit of the Lord will make sure that you do not miss out on receiving your spiritual inheritance.

Begin this journey to destiny today!

Section One

The Voice of the Father

1

Seek the Full Portion!

*A*fter receiving a new heart, that heart must continually be fed by your heavenly Father. Receiving your spiritual inheritance is an ongoing process. You can miss out on all He has for you if you try to diminish this experience by isolating it to a one-time event. Just as you need daily nourishment to keep your physical body alive, you need to be receiving your daily spiritual portion from your heavenly Father to reach your full potential in Christ—to inherit fully the spiritual portion that He has for you.

His portion will change you. It will birth you into destiny. When you are receiving your spiritual portion from God, it will feed your spirit. As your spirit grows, you will come to maturity in Christ. And as Christians everywhere mature in Christ, maturity comes to the body of Christ. So we must be sure we are really getting the Father's portion.

God wants you to receive the full portion of your spiritual inheritance.

I believe a lot of people are asking, even right now, *"Where is my spiritual inheritance?"*

If you are seeking spiritual leadership and nourishment in the body of Christ, your introduction to a local ministry should be based upon a divine connection, communication, and relationship that you have with the leadership of that local ministry. Your connection to that church should not be based upon the choir or the praise and worship team, not upon the basketball club or the usher's board, and not because you like the fact that they throw big birthday parties for their members. In short, you should not join a church for the activities.

Too many people have done this. They have not linked to the divine portion of their spiritual fathers and the deposit of their spiritual mothers, and they have missed out on the spiritual inheritance God has for them.

~

You need to be receiving your daily spiritual portion from your heavenly Father to reach your full potential in Christ.

~

My son, hear the instruction of your father; reject not nor forsake the teaching of your mother. For they are a [victor's] chaplet (garland) of grace upon your head and chains and pendants [of gold worn by kings] for your neck.

—PROVERBS 1:8–9

2

Our Need for Spiritual Leadership

*P*eople—like sheep—must be led. People can easily become entangled with their peers in situations that magnify issues they have not dealt with. They come to church, but their hearts are not in the right posture. Leaders have been called to feed, which means *you must eat.* The Bible's pattern is clear—spiritual leaders are to lead, and we are to submit to their spiritual leadership for spiritual direction.

Spiritual leaders are to lead, and we are to submit to their spiritual leadership for spiritual direction.

The Father's portion is a meal that satisfies, and it must be digested in order to work in our lives. When you walk through the doors of the church, come prepared to worship the Father and receive a meal from His table. A dietician will tell you the best time to eat isn't when you are starving—because you will eat anything. That's our problem. Too many in the body of Christ are starving because we only eat a healthy meal once or twice a week. In other words, we don't maintain intimacy with God on a daily basis, so we can't even digest properly what we receive from Him. We are malnourished.

How can you know when you are receiving your spiritual inheritance? To receive from the Father, you must first be able to acknowledge that God can give your leader the ability to see into your life and to tap into the Spirit. Trust must be developed. But just because you don't have a bond of trust with your leader does not necessarily mean that you need to change churches. *You may simply need to change your posture.* That's what I did. And when I changed, the Spirit of the Lord made sure that I did not miss out on receiving my spiritual inheritance.

~

The Father's portion is a meal that satisfies, and it must be digested in order to work in our lives.

~

Peter…said to Him, Lord, You know everything; You know that I love You [that I have a deep, instinctive, personal affection for You, as for a close friend]. Jesus said to him, Feed My sheep.

—JOHN 21:17

3

The Father's Responsibility

*W*hen I moved to Port Huron, Michigan, it was the beginning of an intense, nine-year process of spiritual growth. God was trying to introduce me to His order, but I couldn't see it because of things that were going on in my life.

I left Port Huron before it was time for me to go, making a move to New York City. When I arrived in New York City, I was impoverished in my spirit and in my bank account. I was going through depression, and my self-esteem had been shot out of the window as the result of some relationships that had not been the will of the Lord for my life. Above this, I was experiencing that "lost feeling" in the church. I had been in church all of my life, yet I still felt as though I didn't really know God. I certainly didn't understand His purpose for saving me.

It is the Father's responsibility to make sure you get your spiritual inheritance.

During these times in New York City I would leave my radio tuned to a gospel station. On one of these occasions I heard Dr. John H. Boyd Sr. speak for the first time. When he began speaking, the power of God literally came through that radio.

My spirit identified with the sound of his voice, but it was something more than just his voice. In the spirit realm it was a sound I recognized, the sound of impartation with a sense of comfort. I felt as if I were in my grandma's kitchen with the smell of apple pie baking in the oven. The sound of Dr. Boyd's voice on the radio that day definitely gave me that "at home" feeling.

I did not yet understand the purpose of spiritual fathers and mothers. I did not know they actually impart our spiritual inheritance from God as they show us His ways and teach us how to respond to Him. I did not have a revelation of this spiritual truth. But God was faithful and made sure I did not miss His portion.

~

I did not yet understand the purpose of spiritual fathers and mothers.

~

But solid food is for full-grown men, for those whose senses and mental faculties are trained by practice to discriminate and distinguish between what is morally good and noble and what is evil and contrary either to divine or human law.

—HEBREWS 5:14

4

Your Father Has a Portion for You

*O*ne Sunday morning I was returning home when one block from home, I noticed a lady standing at a bus stop with three little kids. The Spirit of the Lord said, "Turn around, and ask that lady if she needs a ride."

So I pulled up to the curb. "Ma'am," I said to her, "are you on your way home?"

"No, I'm on my way to church," she told me. "I just missed our church bus, so I'm going to catch the regular bus to church."

The ultimate desire of the Lord is for you to experience true spiritual fatherhood.

"It's really cold out here for your kids," I said. "Are you sure you don't want a ride?" Finally she agreed, saying, "I'll take a ride, if you don't mind."

When we pulled up in front of the church, I wasn't really paying attention to the sign in front of the church. "What is the name of your church?" I asked.

"New Greater Bethel."

The blood rushed to my face. "New Greater Bethel!" I exclaimed. "Dr. John H. Boyd Sr.?"

"Yes! That's my pastor."

It wasn't chance—it was my heavenly Father. I parked my car, walked into the church, and sat in the sixth row from the front on the left side. Pastor Boyd was already preaching his message. Not even ten minutes passed before he looked out into the audience directly at me and said, "Little lady, right there in that uniform. I don't who you are or where you come from. But God told me that you're an eagle with broken wings, and there's a ministry down inside of you. Your worst days are behind you, and your best days are yet to come."

~

It is the responsibility of our heavenly Father to make sure we experience divine fatherhood. This is His gift to us.

~

See what [an incredible] quality of love the Father has given (shown, bestowed on) us, that we should [be permitted to] be named and called and counted the children of God!

—1 JOHN 3:1

5

Come Out of the Wilderness

For much of my life, from the time I left Port Huron until the time God led me to that Sunday morning service at Dr. John Boyd's church, I felt as though I had been wandering in a spiritual desert. No doubt you have experienced your own spiritual wilderness. I believe a wilderness experience is a journey to find our spiritual father. In the midst of my wilderness, God reached out and gave me a spiritual home. The children of Israel wandered in the wilderness until they found their divine place. Egypt wasn't it. Egypt had been their place of bondage. *Remember this:* Any place where you are not receiving the manifold blessings of God is your spiritual Egypt.

> *Any place where you are not receiving the manifold blessings of God is your spiritual Egypt.*

The Israelites belonged to their heavenly Father. Because they were His chosen children, God was obligated to get them out of Egypt. He had a divine place for them—*Canaan*—but they had to go through the wilderness. You know the story.

The vast majority of that first generation never made it to the Promised Land because they were disobedient. A few, however, were brought into their destiny. Joshua and Caleb became leaders for the next generation. They reached the Promised Land.

If you have received Jesus and are still going through that *wilderness experience*, be confident that you belong to God. If He is your heavenly Father, God will make sure you receive His portion. As long as you obey Him, you are destined to find your spiritual parents.

~

I believe a wilderness experience is a journey to find our spiritual father.

~

I brought you into a plentiful land to enjoy its fruits and good things.

—JEREMIAH 2:7

Section Two

The Power of Obedience

6

Serving in the Father's House

The desire to serve is a true sign that you are really *at home*. When you are in the house of your spiritual father, you are not content with being simply a bench member. Natural children have a responsibility to maintain the upkeep of their father's house. In my family,

The desire to serve is a true sign that you are really at home.

we were trained from childhood to wash dishes, vacuum the carpet, clean out the refrigerator, clean out the garbage can, and clean the entire house. We were also trained from childhood that the oldest child is a babysitter for the others. In short, we were taught to look after each other.

There are so many strong comparisons from the natural life of a family to the spiritual. When God demonstrates His love for you by revealing His desire to deepen your relationship with Him through the counsel and teaching of a spiritual father or mother, then you automatically want to show appreciation to God by becoming a servant in the house of your spiritual father or mother.

I believe the first desire of a child of the King is to help build the kingdom of God. This desire comes from the measure of faith you receive from the Father.

To have faith is to have the ability to believe in God. You can believe that He saved you, and you can believe in His workings, because He is faithful. The gift of faith is one of the precious fringe benefits that come along with salvation. At the moment of conversion, you were given faith to build God's kingdom. The Father put a part of Himself into you—and that part wants to manifest according to the abilities God has given you, to serve in His house.

~

Become a servant in the house of your spiritual father or mother.

~

I warn everyone among you...to rate his ability with sober judgment, each according to the degree of faith apportioned by God to him.

—ROMANS 12:3

7

Driven by the Measure of Faith

What we do with the measure of faith God has given us, and the degree to which we use it, is up to us. The Father did not give us a partial measure. Our *degree* of faith is a full measure. It gives us the ability to become faithful, just as God is faithful. When you are operating in the faith of God, you can be faithful to the things of God because you believe in Him. So when you meet your spiritual father, the one whom God has confirmed to you in your spirit, you shouldn't have any problems becoming faithful in your spiritual home. Why? Because you believe in the God of your spiritual father and mother.

When you truly become a child of God, the spirit of a servant becomes one of your first manifestations.

When I joined New Greater Bethel, I knew that I had met the "spiritual father" whom my heavenly Father had prepared for me, because I had an immediate desire to serve in a place I had never been before. My first reaction wasn't, *I don't know these people; I don't know this building. I don't know this church or anything about it.* Immediately my response to God was, "What can I do? Can I sweep, mop, or staple papers? Can I do something to help?"

From the time I started attending Bethel, I was being driven by the measure of faith. I had received a supernatural trust in God, and as a result, I believed He had bestowed upon me a new spiritual father. Immediately, I wanted to do whatever I could to build His kingdom through my church. I wanted God's kingdom to become great because of what I had been given.

~

Our degree of faith is a full measure. It gives us the ability to become faithful, just as God is faithful.

~

Whoever desires to be great among you must be your servant, and whoever wishes to be most important and first in rank among you must be slave of all.

—MARK 10:43–44

Your Measure Is Your Spiritual Assignment

*O*ne of the first signs that you are in the right spiritual home is when your spirit becomes humbled to the point that you ask, "What can I do?" In John 4:34, Jesus said, "My food (nourishment) is to do the will (pleasure) of Him Who sent Me and to accomplish and completely finish His work." Jesus did everything according to the Father's will. His heartbeat was to make sure He fulfilled His Father's assignment.

> *One of the first signs that you are in the right spiritual home is when your spirit becomes humbled to the point that you ask, "What can I do?"*

God gives our leaders a vision, a purpose, and a plan—and then He births children into the kingdom who are capable of helping them to fulfill it. For example, if your spiritual father's assignment is to paint the largest mural in New York City, then the heavenly Father will send him children who can help him to fulfill the vision.

This reveals another way you can know when you are in the right place. Whatever the vision of your father is, you have been equipped with a calling, gifts, and talents that correspond to his vision. What does this mean? The anointing you have is not for you. It is to make sure the vision your heavenly Father has given to your spiritual father and mother will be fulfilled.

Many Christians don't have a revelation of this. We think our job is simply to sing in the choir or to be an usher. We don't understand that we are an intricate part of the puzzle that moves a vision forward and causes it to flourish. The measure of faith we have been given—along with our spiritual gifts—*becomes* our spiritual assignment.

~

The anointing you have is to make sure the vision your heavenly Father has given to your spiritual father and mother will be fulfilled.

~

Jesus said to them, My food (nourishment) is to do the will (pleasure) of Him Who sent Me and to accomplish and completely finish His work.

—JOHN 4:34

9

There Is Power in Obedience

Obedience is vital to your walk with God. Jesus came in the form of a Son, in order to redeem man back to God. This was the only way that the Father's vision could be fulfilled. As a Son, Christ remained in complete obedience to the Father's vision. Hear me. Jesus did not come with His own vision. He did not come with His own plan. When He was sitting in glory with the heavenly Father, they looked out over the world and saw sin and degradation.

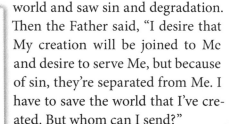

True sons and daughters in the kingdom are focused on the will and vision of their spiritual fathers.

Then the Father said, "I desire that My creation will be joined to Me and desire to serve Me, but because of sin, they're separated from Me. I have to save the world that I've created. But whom can I send?"

Jesus said, "I'll go." And when He came, it wasn't to start His own ministry. He came to build the kingdom of God; He came to fulfill His Father's vision. Everything Jesus said and did constantly referred people back to the Father.

True sons and daughters in the kingdom are focused on the will and vision of their spiritual fathers. But can we obey as Jesus did? Yes! Because Jesus said, "He who believes in Me [who cleaves to and trusts in and relies on Me] as the Scripture has said, From his innermost being shall flow [continuously] springs and rivers of living water" (John 7:38).

Rivers of living water flow out of us because they have flowed into us from somewhere else. In other words, there are no "original" anointings. The apostle Paul illustrates this point with his words: "I planted, Apollos watered, but God [all the while] was making it grow and [He] gave the increase" (1 Cor. 3:6). Some people are called to water, others are called to plant, but it is God who brings the increase.

> God is calling you to a spiritual vision that is being passed from generation to generation.

He who believes in Me [who cleaves to and trusts in and relies on Me] as the Scripture has said, From his innermost being shall flow [continuously] springs and rivers of living water.

—JOHN 7:38

10

Following the Example of Christ

*J*esus entered the world wrapped in the blanket of time and a fleshly body (which had a time limit on it), and then He died.

Paul could affirm that he lived by faith in Christ's sacrifice (Gal. 2:20), and we can affirm it, because of Jesus. Christ was so determined to finish the Father's will that He gave up the fleshly frame, which hindered the full expression of His obedience. He released Himself unto death so that He would be able to live inside of every living being that would believe on Him—regardless of the time or place.

> *Jesus released Himself unto death so that He would be able to live inside of every living being that would believe on Him—regardless of the time or place.*

When we believe in the Lord and in the workings of the Father—who sent the Son—we can fulfill His vision and will because Christ lives in us. Salvation isn't only for our benefit (though we benefit by being saved from hell and gaining a heavenly position). While we live in these fleshly frames, we have the ultimate goal of finishing the will of the Father—because Jesus is working in us (Phil. 2:13). His number one goal will never change. He will never stop until the Father's plan is complete.

The power of submission and obedience to our spiritual parents is much deeper than just saying, "He's my pastor" or "She's my pastor." We are part of a vision that is much greater than anything we know. When we disobey and don't submit to the Father's will, then we hinder His plan and crucify Christ afresh according to Hebrews 6:4–8. This binds Him to the state of being crucified, which means we haven't released Him to His supernatural ministry—fulfilling the will of the Father in our life.

> While we live in these fleshly frames, we have the ultimate goal of finishing the will of the Father.

> I have been crucified with Christ [in Him I have shared His crucifixion]; it is no longer I who live, but Christ (the Messiah) lives in me.
>
> —GALATIANS 2:20

11

Don't Get Disgruntled

The body of Christ hasn't reached the purpose of doing the Father's will because we stay too offended to build His kingdom. Our attention stays focused on what's being done to us in the fleshly realm. To be honest with you, the only way we can prove authentically that we are the body of Christ is to have scars. If we are His body, then we have to have nail prints. We have to be whipped, spat upon, and talked about to be authentic sons and daughters.

The only way we can prove authentically that we are the body of Christ is to have scars.

You will have to go through some things, walk through difficult situations, and deal with hard issues—things the enemy tries to use to wipe you out—and still survive, because you belong to the body of Christ. You survive because you belong to the Father and obey the Son, doing what He called, anointed, and appointed you to do. You survive by activating your "measure of faith."

The most important part of us is being renewed—the spiritual part that fulfills the plan of the Father—so that we can build the kingdom.

Every vision that God has given to His leaders is part of the puzzle. No two churches are supposed to be alike. They are not supposed to have the same ministry! Some churches have drug ministries, some have soup kitchen ministries, others have hospital ministries, and so on.

Don't get disgruntled at the vision of your spiritual father. We are all here to do one thing, and that is to build the kingdom of God.

Faithfulness can only be birthed in a person when he or she is willing to obey the voice of the Father, no matter what the price. There is power in obedience.

~

The way we obtain the respect of having a ministry is by being faithful to that which belongs to our spiritual father.

~

Though our outer man is [progressively] decaying and wasting away, yet our inner self is being [progressively] renewed day after day.

—2 CORINTHIANS 4:16

12

Obedience Is Taught

The Bible says that Jesus was a miracle worker. He opened blind eyes and cast out devils—but there was one thing He had to be taught. Hebrews 5:8 says, "Although He was a Son, He learned [active, special] obedience through what He suffered." Obedience to the Father's will brought power to His name.

Too many of us are trying to build a name. People are

Unless you have walked in your own obedience and fulfilled it— then you lose power and authority.

running around in the body of Christ doing things and establishing things that God never told them to do—because they are trying to build a name. Listen to me. This isn't how you get a name! You will get a name when you establish and respect the workings of your father.

Your name will never be empowered unless you operate under the authority of your spiritual parents, unless you suffer in obedience to gain power!

That's why demons became subject to Jesus! He could command their obedience because His obedience was complete. This is also why many are ministering but have no power. They failed the test of obedience. Unless you have walked in your own obedience and fulfilled it—meaning you have obeyed everything God has told you to do—then you lose power and authority.

Now, we are waiting for the greatest revival ever to hit this country. And it will never happen in its fullness until the body of Christ comes into a state of readiness, like Jesus. When our own submission and obedience as a church are fully secured and complete, awesome power will be released. We have no power because we have no obedience. We are not willing for our flesh to suffer in order to fulfill the Father's will.

~

When our own submission and obedience as a church are fully secured and complete, awesome power will be released.

~

[His completed experience] making Him perfectly [equipped], He became the Author and Source of eternal salvation to all those who give heed and obey Him.

—HEBREWS 5:9

13

Coming Into Spiritual Order

$\mathcal{G}$od designed His plan so that we would walk in spiritual order. Before you can even understand God, you have to go through spiritual order. For example, God didn't send the children of Israel rampaging out of Egypt. He gave them a leader to get them out. And when that leader disobeyed Him, He gave them another leader to take them into the Promised Land. *Leading is God's way.*

When you exchange the manservant of God for an image—a tie, a suit, an office, and a title—then you will never reach your divine destiny.

When you look at it, it didn't matter how much the children of Israel cried out to God; nothing happened for them until Moses went before the Father. When Moses said, "They're hungry," that's when the quail fell (Num. 11:21–22, 31). When Moses said, "They're thirsty," the people got water (Exod. 17:3–7; Num. 20:2–11). When Moses held up his arms, the Red Sea opened up (Exod. 14:21–22).

Too many Christians are at the end of their roads and can't go any further because a "Red Sea" is in front of them.

And the reason we are not crossing over—while the enemy is behind us jumping all over our backs, tearing up our houses, our marriages, and our children—is that we don't have a leader to hold his hands up on our behalf. Too many believers don't have a spiritual father. Hear me. If you are going to accomplish anything for God, you have to be in divine order.

~

If you are going to accomplish anything for God, you have to be in divine order.

~

And His gifts were [varied; He Himself appointed and gave men to us]....His intention was the perfecting and the full equipping of the saints (His consecrated people), [that they should do] the work of ministering toward building up Christ's body (the church).

—Ephesians 4:11–12

14

Embrace Authority

*G*od's way is the leader way. Throughout the history of the Bible, from beginning to end, God always used a leader to bring victory to His people. When you acknowledge someone else's authority, it means this person has the power and the right to give orders and make decisions. When you respect the authority that has been placed over your life, you don't have to wander in the valley of decision. You don't have to be without direction—because God has given someone the right to give orders and make decisions that cover you. He can order the enemy out of your life, and he can unlock your destiny.

We are empowered by submission.

A person has authority in the spirit realm because he or she is living in submission to the Father. Therefore, a leader who is doing the will of the Father has this God-given grace. And for this reason, you should willingly comply with his or her direction. Your pastor has the right to say, "I want you to be in Tuesday night service every week. Don't you miss a service."

In essence, every leader walks under the same principle as every son and daughter. Nobody escapes the process of obedience and submission. God is the ultimate authority. He is every leader's authority, and our leaders are our authorities. There are also authority structures in our homes. In everything and in every area of our lives, our spirits and everything in the flesh must submit under the authority and power of God.

We are empowered by submission. When we submit to authority in obedience to God, then we have the power to command the enemy. We have power over anything that comes to attack or destroy our destiny.

~

When you respect the authority that has been placed over your life, you don't have to wander in the valley of decision.

~

Let every person be loyally subject to the governing (civil) authorities. For there is no authority except from God [by His permission, His sanction], and those that exist do so by God's appointment.

—ROMANS 13:1

15

The Principle of Satan

When Satan was still called *Lucifer*, he was in the heavenlies serving God. Every being knew he was a worshiper; his whole being was built to worship God. But the Book of Isaiah says he wanted to become "equal" with God. He said in his heart, "I will ascend to heaven; I will exalt my throne above the stars of God; I will sit upon the mount of assembly in the uttermost north. I will ascend above the heights of the clouds; I will make myself like the Most High" (Isa. 14:13–14).

Anything that is operating in the I realm is in the flesh realm.

The minute Lucifer began the whole *I* thing, he became an individual without God. Hear me. The power of the Godhead is in the Trinity: Father, Son, and Holy Spirit. The conversation of Christ is always *We*, *Us*, and *Our*. So whenever you hear a person say "I," he or she is canceling out the principle of God and is disconnected from the source of power. Anything that is operating in the *I* realm is in the flesh realm. And anything that is in the flesh realm was born into the world in a state of deterioration.

The enemy is not afraid of a person who preaches. He is not afraid of our messages! He is not scared of the person who is shouting and speaking in tongues in church. He is not even threatened by someone who can quote the Bible verbatim, from cover to cover. But he is terrified of the person who has submitted his life under the obedience of Christ. Satan is petrified of obedience, because an obedient person knows how to follow the orders of the Lord. God's order says, "Let God arise, let his enemies be scattered" (Ps. 68:1, KJV).

The enemy is terrified of the person who has submitted his life under the obedience of Christ.

I have been crucified with Christ [in Him I have shared His crucifixion]; it is no longer I who live, but Christ (the Messiah) lives in me; and the life I now live in the body I live by faith in (by adherence to and reliance on and complete trust in) the Son of God, Who loved me and gave Himself up for me.

—GALATIANS 2:20

16

You Need to Obey

We were consecrated, sanctified, and made holy by the Spirit for the purpose of being obedient to Jesus Christ and sprinkled with His blood.

We were chosen and foreknown by God the Father, and then consecrated, sanctified, and made holy by the Spirit. Then we are to be obedient to Jesus Christ and be sprinkled with His blood. Only when these actions have been taken can we move to the next part of this spiritual principle.

If you are constantly walking in disobedience, then the plan of salvation is missing from your life.

Most of the things we are battling against in the body of Christ, and trying to keep ourselves free from, come along with—*are fringe benefits of*—being obedient to Christ! In our obedience to Christ, blessings are increased, and our peace is increased *in abundance*. When we realize all of these things come through Christ and being obedient to Him, we can be *free indeed*.

The favor of the Lord rests upon you when you understand that you have been saved, sanctified, and consecrated to obey. There is power in obedience!

You don't need to pray for peace, because peace comes with obedience. You don't need to pray for abundance. Abundance comes with obedience. You don't have to pray for favor. Favor comes with obedience. And you don't have to fight the devil to keep from sinning, because deliverance from the fear of *agitating passions* and *moral misconduct* comes with obeying. Oh, yes, there is power in obedience.

~

The favor of the Lord rests upon you when you understand that you have been saved, sanctified, and consecrated to obey. There is power in obedience!

~

...[Born anew] into an inheritance which is beyond the reach of change and decay [imperishable], unsullied and unfading, reserved in heaven for you, who are being guarded (garrisoned) by God's power through [your] faith [till you fully inherit that final] salvation that is ready to be revealed [for you] in the last time.

—1 Peter 1:4–5

Section Three

Receiving the Father's Portion

17

Spiritual Fathers Lead to Spiritual Inheritance

*W*hen you get all the way back to the beginning of your life in Christ, back to where you first were born in Him, most likely you will find that you followed the same pattern as Saul—you started out as a nobody. First Samuel 9:2 says that Saul was the son of Kish. Other than being very handsome, he hadn't done anything great. He was just the son of a Benjamite.

His encounter with his spiritual father showed him the purpose for his life.

As the story of Saul's encounter with Samuel begins, Saul was going to look for donkeys in obedience to his natural father. In his pursuit to obey his father, he and the servant stayed out looking for so long that he finally said to the servant, "Maybe we ought to go back so my father won't worry about us." (See verses 3–5.)

His servant said, "Behold now, there is in this city a man of God, a man held in honor; all that he says surely comes true. Now let us go there. Perhaps he can show us where we should go" (v. 6). This demonstrates how important it is to be careful about the people you run with. Note this important principle. Saul's father sent two men: one was a *son*, and the other was a *servant*. The son was in *obedience*, and the servant understood *authority*.

Since the servant understood authority, he provoked the son to stay in obedience. When Saul was ready to give up, the servant said, "Let's keep looking for the donkeys." If Saul had not stayed in obedience, if he had given up his search and returned to his father, he would not have found Samuel. He may not have encountered the spiritual father who could lead him into his spiritual inheritance.

Let's understand something: Saul came to Samuel looking for donkeys, not to be anointed as king of Israel. His encounter with his spiritual father showed him the purpose for his life.

~

If Saul had not stayed in obedience, he may not have encountered the spiritual father who could lead him into his spiritual inheritance.

~

The servant said to him, Behold now, there is in this city a man of God, a man held in honor; all that he says surely comes true. Now let us go there. Perhaps he can show us where we should go.

—1 SAMUEL 9:6

18

Entering Into Purpose

When you come into the knowledge of your spiritual parents, you will come with a vision, a goal, and a desire—but they are going to give you destiny. You will come to them with one purpose, and because of their nature as spiritual parents, they will introduce you to your destiny, because *they know* you don't know it. You are too busy doing the "work of the church," but your spiritual parents are called to show you the purpose of your life.

> When you come into the knowledge of your spiritual parents, you will come with a vision, a goal, and a desire— but they are going to give you destiny.

Saul was looking for donkeys that he couldn't even find. His heavenly Father brought him to the man of God who would prepare him for his destiny!

The man or woman of God can anoint you for your purpose. You can't do it! You can't even find donkeys by yourself. You don't have enough discernment in your spirit to even know where they might be. But a person who is under the obedience of God, under a mighty anointing, can see in the Spirit, lay hands on you, and anoint you for a worldwide, universal call.

Why does God do things this way? He does it because He hears the cry of His people, and because of that cry, He calls into destiny the answer to His people's cry. He does this by picking out people who don't know how to fulfill His purposes. He sends them to anointed leaders who will anoint those people into something greater than either of them can control—destiny. He will do this with you if you allow Him to. He will send you to your spiritual father or mother who will anoint you for your spiritual destiny. But both you and your spiritual leader must seek the Lord constantly to avoid messing up this mantle.

⁓

How do you know your future spiritual father? Two things: You will eat what he feeds you. He will be able to discern your spirit.

⁓

He who is faithful in a very little [thing] is faithful also in much, and he who is dishonest and unjust in a very little [thing] is dishonest and unjust also in much.

—LUKE 16:10

19

Discovering True Riches

*W*hen Saul confronted Samuel, Samuel also addressed the matter of the lost donkeys. He said to Saul, "As for your donkeys that were lost three days ago, do not be thinking about them, for they are found" (1 Sam. 9:20). Samuel knew things about Saul that he could not have known in the natural.

> *It is the divine revelation given to our leaders that enables us to reach our divine destinies—because we cannot see destiny.*

After confirming to Saul that his father's donkeys had been found, Samuel raised Saul's vision to the bigger picture of his spiritual inheritance. In other words, a spiritual father raises your vision. He moved Saul's thinking from donkeys to destiny.

What about all of the stuff that's going on in your family—your mother, father, sisters, brothers, finances, emotions...marriage? God sent Jesus to give you authority in those areas. When your spiritual father finds you, he will anoint you to receive victory over everything that threatens to hurt your family or to destroy your lineage.

This is the real purpose for which you need a spiritual father. God has introduced you to a spiritual father so that through him the Lord can draw you into destiny.

In the story of Saul and Samuel we can identify the way to know when you have met your spiritual authority. You will know because it will require an act of obedience on your part to respond to what your spiritual father says to you. It required Saul's obedience for him to respond to the words of Samuel.

It is the divine revelation given to our leaders that enables us to reach our divine destinies—because we cannot see destiny.

~

God has introduced you to a spiritual father so that through him the Lord can draw you into destiny.

~

When Samuel saw Saul, the Lord told him, There is the man of whom I told you. He shall have authority over My people.

—1 SAMUEL 9:17

20

The Portion Reserved for You

*A*nother illustration can be drawn from 1 Samuel 9:21. In essence, Saul was saying to Samuel, "Why are you speaking such powerful and deep things to me? You're saying I'm going to be a deliverer over Israel when I'm just a Benjamite. I'm just Kish's son. Nobody in my family has that kind of calling on their lives." This shows us that when we are brought into purpose, and our leaders reveal who we are, then we have to be taught who we really are. We have to be trained according to the vision of those God has placed over us. If not, we would be limited by our own capacity.

When God has revealed to our leaders who we are in the Spirit, then our feedings will lead us to where we are going.

When God has revealed to our leaders who we are in the Spirit, then our feedings will lead us to where we are going. In other words, this new spiritual food shouldn't be reduced to being something "common." As their spiritual children, we must be able to go to new levels in God, to the level of our spiritual parents. We must adapt our appetite and learn to digest the same meat.

Listen to me. This means that the things God has in store for you will happen when you show up. So you have to be in divine obedience to not miss your divine connection—because before you get there, the atmosphere is already being prepared. The meal has been reserved. It was handpicked before you came.

That's why when you come to a church, and God divinely connects you with a ministry, you feel as if you have been there for years. It seems that you have known the pastor for a long time, because the Lord has already revealed in the spirit realm that you are coming. The atmosphere has been prepared. That's why you can sit down when you first walk into a church and say, "Wow, that was just what I needed." The Holy Spirit knew you were coming, and He had reserved the portion made ready for you.

~

The things God has in store for you will happen when you show up.

~

[Samuel] said, See what was reserved for you.
—1 SAMUEL 9:24

21

Wait on God's Timing

When you have met your spiritual father, and he begins to impart that divine assignment into your life, it will require a change in some of your relationships. On the second day of Saul's visit with him, Samuel spoke these words to Saul: "Get up, that I may send you on your way" (1 Sam. 9:26). As they walked through the outskirts of the city, Samuel said to Saul, "Bid the servant pass on before us—and he passed on—but you stand still, first, that I may cause you to hear the word of God" (v. 27).

We "go" before our time instead of waiting on the timing of the Lord.

No doubt you will need to let some people "pass on before you" also so that you can "stand still…to hear the word of God." People who started out with you won't be the ones you end up with. Samuel told him, "Send the servant on, because this isn't for his ears. This isn't his divine appointment. He just happened to be with you; but you stand still, because before I send you, I have to tell you what God is saying over your life."

This is where many of us miss the mark. We meet the right divine connection, we are in the right church, and we have the right pastor—but we don't wait on the word of God. We are not still enough so that the full word of the Lord concerning our life can be imparted unto us. So we "go" before our time instead of waiting on the timing of the Lord. We begin to operate by association. This is false authority.

In short, we think we have arrived. The fact is, we have moved out before our time. We left before we were *still enough* to hear the word of the Lord and receive His true assignment for our lives. The *full portion* of the Lord is your spiritual inheritance…you just have to wait for God's timing.

~

We meet the right divine connection, we are in the right church, and we have the right pastor—but we don't wait on the word of God.

~

Giving thanks to the Father, Who has qualified and made us fit to share the portion which is the inheritance of the saints (God's holy people) in the Light.

—COLOSSIANS 1:12

True Riches Are in Your Father's House

The principle of waiting on God's timing is illustrated in the story of the prodigal son in Luke 15:11–32. He lived in his father's house and, like his brothers, had an inheritance. He knew who he was, that he was above the servants—but he made a mistake. He began to ask for the physical portion of his inheritance without understanding who he was in the Spirit. We do this all the time today. We want to drive the same kinds of cars our pastors are driving. We want to wear the same kinds of clothes. We want to preach using their body gestures. We want to sound like them and move in the Spirit like they do.

We have to be careful that we are not forcing our spiritual fathers to give us a physical inheritance, while at the same time we are missing who we are in the Spirit.

The story of the prodigal son shows us that at times it takes losing a physical inheritance to gain your spiritual destiny. The prodigal son actually took his inheritance and wasted it by going into the world and trying it out on his own. Then he realized his error. He came back home and said, "I missed God. I missed it altogether."

Then he said something even more profound: "I'd rather be a servant in my father's house. If I could just go back and become a servant." (See Luke 15:19.) He had to swallow the fact that he had wasted his physical inheritance. As a result, he was able to understand the significance of being in his father's house. This was a valuable lesson. He had come to the place where he valued being in his father's house more than what he had in his hand.

~

You will never get to your next level until you are willing to give up those who think you are wonderful in order to stand in the presence of somebody who can discern what you need.

~

Then Samuel took the vial of oil and poured it on Saul's head and kissed him and said, Has not the Lord anointed you to be prince over His heritage Israel?

—1 Samuel 10:1

Section Four

The Anointing: Divine Order

23

Experiencing the Anointing

*W*hen you truly meet your divine connection, that person will have the anointing to help resolve your past while ushering you into the future. When Saul encountered Samuel, Samuel did much more than tell him where to look for his father's donkeys. Samuel initiated the flow of spiritual inheritance into the life of Saul. (See 1 Samuel 10:2–6.)

In six verses, from the time Samuel said, "Stand still and let me tell you what the will of God is for your life," Saul was transformed from a man chasing donkeys into a blessed prophet. His physical needs were met; a divine assignment was spoken over his life; he was anointed for that assignment; and with one prophecy, one kiss, and one vial of oil, he was turned into a different man. The same prophetic gift that was upon Samuel instantly came upon Saul.

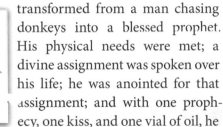

Your spiritual father will always work to get you in the right atmosphere.

Saul never had to be birthed out into the prophetic. He had never lived in the tabernacle to learn the voice of God on his own. He simply had to stand still and let the man of God reveal the word of the Lord over his life. And in six verses he received an anointing, provision, and divine placement in the right company. One man of God changed everything about his life.

Too many of us are in the right place under the right leader, but we haven't allowed *that leader* to find us the *right company*. It is as though Samuel was saying, "In order to walk in this assignment, you're going to have to change your company. You have to get among the kind of people that have the same kind of anointing. And you're going to know who they are, because first of all, they're going to be coming down from a high place."

Your spiritual father will always work to get you in the right atmosphere. He will get you in a place where the Spirit of the Lord is moving all the time, with people who will have like spirits and the same anointing.

~

When you truly meet your divine connection, that person will have the anointing to help resolve your past while ushering you into the future.

~

Then the Spirit of the Lord will come upon you mightily, and you will show yourself to be a prophet with them; and you will be turned into another man.

—1 SAMUEL 10:6

24

Can God Trust You?

*G*od is saying that before you can be birthed out from your leader, several things need to take place. Your leaders have to watch you separate yourself from anything that is less than you are. And they have to find out whether or not you are able to follow instructions. After Samuel anointed and kissed Saul, there were several instructions from Samuel that Saul could not afford to miss.

First of all, you have to be taught and instructed. Your leaders have to see you follow instructions. This starts immediately after you are called and anointed. When Samuel gave instructions to Saul in 1 Samuel 10:2, Saul had to go to Rachel's tomb. He couldn't go where he wanted to go. He couldn't go to the left side of the mountain. He had to go exactly where Samuel told him to go. He had been anointed, kissed, and given the word of the Lord. It was a new day. Samuel had revealed to Saul who he was going to become.

> *"Can I trust you not to take advantage of this situation?"*

Samuel said, "You're going to meet three men. Together, they will be carrying three kids, three loaves, and a skin of wine. Can I trust you not to take more than what you need? Can I trust you with offerings? Can I trust you not to take advantage of this situation?"

Can your spiritual father trust you when he is not around? Can he trust you not to be manipulative? Can he trust you to take only what he told you to take   that even though there are a host of things you could probably take, you choose to uphold his word and follow instructions? Can he trust you to keep your divine assignment to yourself until the time appointed?

~

Can your spiritual father trust you when he is not around?

~

Elisha said to him, Did not my spirit go with you when the man turned from his chariot to meet you? Was it a time to accept money, garments, olive orchards, vineyards, sheep, oxen, menservants, and maidservants? Therefore the leprosy of Naaman shall cleave to you and to your offspring forever. And Gehazi went from his presence a leper as white as snow.

—2 KINGS 5:26–27

25

Keep It to Yourself

*T*here is another spiritual principle we must learn from the story of Saul's introduction to spiritual destiny. Christians need to learn how not to become braggadocios toward people in their circle of influence who have not been called to the same level of destiny.

In 1 Samuel 10:14–16, Saul illustrates a level of spiritual understanding that young Joseph failed to grasp. Joseph got himself in trouble because the Lord had revealed his destiny in a dream, but he spoke it at the wrong time, in the wrong place, and in the wrong way. He walked over to his brothers and said, "I had a dream that I was going to be over all of you, and that you are all going to be my servants."

Regardless of the circumstances, it is your leader's responsibility to make an announcement about you.

(See Genesis 37.) These statements gave him a pit experience.

Joseph became a braggadocio. He was almost rubbing it in his brothers' faces that God had a call upon his life! So he had to go by way of the pit so that God could purify his gift.

Joseph had to develop character and learn obedience through suffering so that the mantle God had placed upon him could become a blessing to his family—not a knife in their sides. When you lack wisdom, and when you speak those things that were spoken to you in private, it can cause your journey to divine destiny to be painful. This happens when your motive is not spiritual growth—instead it is self-recognition.

I believe the whole process of Samuel giving Saul instructions and telling him how to handle himself reveals another important lesson. In the midst of receiving a great anointing, Saul had to be taught balance. He had to receive wisdom in the area of his new anointing.

~

Christians have announced themselves and proclaimed their own importance instead of acting in humility.

~

Do not boast of [yourself and] tomorrow, for you know not what a day may bring forth. Let another man praise you, and not your own mouth; a stranger, and not your own lips.

—PROVERBS 27:1–2

26

The Test of Character

$\mathscr{A}$t every divine turn in our lives, we must be corrected in our character. We must not be allowed to get away with anything once we have received the mantle and anointing for a divine assignment. The Bible says, "A little leaven leaveneth the whole lump" (Gal. 5:9, KJV). Before you know it, a little lying will lead to a lot of lying; a little cheating will lead to a lot of cheating; and a little stealing will lead to a whole lot of stealing. The flesh has to be cut.

Your divine purpose can only be established by counsel.

The portion God wants us to receive isn't material wealth. He is trying to walk us through the process of inheriting morality, stability, integrity, and right standing with God and man from our spiritual parents.

After we have received our father's mantle of the anointing, we must become spiritual children—daughters of Zion and sons of thunder—and be willing to submit to instruction.

There are many in the body of Christ who have had great anointings placed upon them, but they are beating the air with no aim. We cannot war after our own purposes. We cannot war for our destiny. We cannot war for our spiritual assignments without counsel, because it is through counsel that the purposes and plans of the Father are established.

The anointing alone doesn't establish our purposes. Our destiny cannot be established from just having a "high time" in church. It can't be established from goose bumps and tears. These things are only the beginning. Your divine purpose can only be established by counsel, or else you will be fighting without aim. When you walk without the counsel and instruction of a spiritual father, the devil is going to wear you out.

~

God is trying to walk us through the process of inheriting morality, stability, integrity, and right standing with God and man.

~

Purposes and plans are established by counsel; and [only] with good advice make or carry on war.

—PROVERBS 20:18

Section Five

*S*tepping Over Authority

27

Staying Under Authority

One of the major problems in the kingdom of God is not the failure to anoint people *into* positions, but instead, in teaching or training them how to *stay in their grace*. People need to know how to stay in position.

When Saul was anointed to become king over Israel, God began to use him, and he stepped among the prophets as Samuel had commanded. Then he began to speak as the prophets did. In doing so, Saul stepped into an anointing that he didn't have prior to that experience. When he went in among these mighty men and prophets, Saul started prophesying to the point that people who had known him didn't even recognize who he was. The anointing literally changed Saul into a different man.

Because of His submission to God, Jesus had access to everything that belonged to the Father, and God was able to use Him in mighty ways.

This can also serve as a warning. Why? Knowing the story of Saul, we must be careful that upon being changed into another man, we don't assume false authority. In other words, when someone anoints you, you don't become *that* person. You become a partaker of his or her grace.

While Jesus was in the earth realm, He said that everything He did was done to glorify His Father—not to glorify Himself (though the Father was using Him powerfully to get the work done). He always pointed the attention and the respect back to His heavenly Father. He always acknowledged the fact that the anointing in which He operated belonged to the Father. He did this because He was submitted. Please get this! Because of His submission to God, Jesus had access to everything that belonged to the Father, and God was able to use Him in mighty ways.

~

> When God uses a man or woman of God to place an anointing upon you, the next step of receiving that anointing is to come under submission.

~

> Although He was a Son, He learned [active, special] obedience through what He suffered.
>
> —Hebrews 5:8

28

Pride Will Bring Disobedience

At the beginning of 1 Samuel 13, Saul began his reign as king of Israel. At this point of his reign, the children of Israel were about to go to battle, and they found themselves in a tight situation. They were outnumbered by their enemies, and they were shaking and trembling as they followed Saul. Samuel had required that Saul wait for him for seven days in Gilgal until the appointed time. But when the seven days had

To be in obedience means to be in compliance with someone else's wishes or orders.

passed, Samuel had not yet arrived, and the people were scattering. Saul was in fear and felt that he must do something, *right then—with or without Samuel.*

Pride convinces you that your spirit is in a certain place and, as a result, you can walk in that place doing things God has not authorized you to do. This is what happened to Saul. He reacted to the people's actions and took that step out of authority: "So Saul said, Bring me the burnt offering and the peace offerings. And he offered the burnt offering [which he was forbidden to do]" (1 Sam. 13:9).

Saul wasn't a priest! And because he wasn't a priest, he couldn't function in the office of a prophet (though he had received a prophetic anointing from Samuel). In short, Saul was not ordained by God to step into that position. When Samuel found out what Saul had done, he said, "You have done foolishly! You have not kept the commandment of the Lord your God which He commanded you; for the Lord would have established your kingdom over Israel forever" (v. 13).

Obedience runs like a golden cord throughout this entire book. When we walk in obedience to God and yield to the will of others (i.e., our spiritual leadership), then we are truly submitting to His authority.

⁓

When your ministry, anointing, and the work you believe God has called you to do is about you, it will force you to step out of the will of God.

⁓

Samuel said to Saul, You have done foolishly! You have not kept the commandment of the Lord your God which He commanded you; for the Lord would have established your kingdom over Israel forever.

—1 SAMUEL 13:13

29

Learning Submission

*T*he Holy Spirit, the Spirit of Truth, transmits everything to us in perfect divine order...so you must be willing to receive from those who carry His authority on earth. You must be in compliance with what God says and prophesies to you through your spiritual fathers, so that when they lay hands on you, you will receive the imparted anointing to operate in the calling and purpose of God.

> *Many people have made submission a matter of submission to a person; they have not understood that submission is a matter of submitting to the authority of God.*

Many people have made submission a matter of submission to *a person*; they have not understood that submission is a matter of submitting to *the authority of God*. Submission is about the incorruptible portion we are trying to obtain from our heavenly Father.

Submission is about what I am trained *into*. In other words, it is about what God is training me to do. For me, I know He is training and positioning my spirit so that I can be an oil carrier and, even more, the carrier of a mantle that goes beyond the body of Christ. I want to be able to transmit this weight of authority, this anointing that I have been given, into somebody else's life. Therefore, I must be willing to pass every test of obedience.

Jesus understood that if He continued the process of obedience and submission—and respected, recognized, and acknowledged the authority of the One that was over Him—He was well on the way to gain power. Hear me. Being able to walk in the power and authority of God is our ultimate goal. We miss it when we become entangled in the flesh. That's why the Bible says we must submit to one to another, because submission keeps the anointing oil flowing down into your life.

~

The way to ultimate power is through the direction of divine counsel.

~

Where there is no counsel, purposes are frustrated, but with many counselors they are accomplished.

—PROVERBS 15:22

30

Consequences of Disobedience

*R*egardless of how high you go in ministry, no matter how high your calling and title may be, God requires you to be submitted and accountable. Even the president of the United States cannot function in this capacity alone. He has to be accountable. He has to submit himself to others who are more knowledgeable than he is in specific areas. If he is going to rule the most powerful nation in the world, he must do this. Oh, yes! The law of authority can be seen in every area of life.

The law of authority can be seen in every area of life.

God did not waste any time in dealing with Saul's disobedience. Right after Saul offered the sacrifice, Samuel showed up with a spiritual reprimand for Saul's foolish disobedience. It brought serious consequences (1 Sam. 13:13–14). When Saul numbered the people that were left with him, he found out that there were only about six hundred left (v. 15).

Saul started out with thousands and ended up with six hundred. This is what happens when you begin to walk in disobedience and step over the authority God has given you. Instead of gaining, you lose. At first, you look like a great wonder, but it all begins to diminish—because only the authentic oil of the anointing causes multiplication. The oil of the anointing causes you to prosper. What the Lord allows to be spoken and poured into your life by your spiritual father is what causes your tent to be expanded. The Bible tells us to broaden our horizons, enlarge our territories, and expand our tents—but it has to flow down God's way.

If you can't house and digest the anointing of your spiritual father, then you won't have strength to put out anything of substance. Your body will be weak, and your ministry will be weak. When the anointing on your life is weak, the gifts in which you operate will be anemic.

~

When you begin to walk in disobedience and step over the authority God has given you, instead of gaining, you lose.

~

Samuel said, Has the Lord as great a delight in burnt offerings and sacrifices as in obeying the voice of the Lord? Behold, to obey is better than sacrifice, and to hearken than the fat of rams.

—1 Samuel 15:22

31

Fallout in the Chain of Command

*W*hen Samuel discovered Saul's disobedience, he spoke a word to Saul to tell him that he had lost his kingdom forever and that the Lord had chosen someone else who would obey Him. Yet Saul moved on and started regathering his army, trying to pull it all back together. But it wasn't easy. The Philistines had surrounded the Israelites on three sides, and they had killed or taken captive every metal worker in the land of Israel. Afraid that the Israelites would make swords and spears to fight against them, the Philistines forced the Israelites to come to them and pay a price to have their plowshares, mattocks, axes, and sickles sharpened. And of course the Philistines did not do a good job of sharpening these tools. On the day of battle, none of the Israelites had swords or spears to carry except for Saul and his son Jonathan. (See 1 Samuel 13:16–23.)

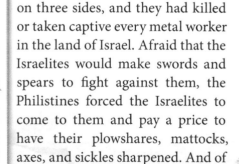

Jonathan had already assumed his father's authority in just the same way his father had taken Samuel's authority. The process did not stop with Saul.

Even though Saul had been informed by Samuel that he had lost his kingdom through disobedience, he refused to give it up, continuing in his disobedient spirit. And it wasn't long before Saul's chain of command was affected by this same spirit. Even his son Jonathan displayed a disobedient spirit. "One day Jonathan son of Saul said to his armour-bearer, Come, let us go over to the Philistine garrison on the other side. But he did not tell his father" (1 Sam. 14:1).

The process of disobedience did not stop with Saul; it moved from Saul to his son Jonathan. And it would not stop there. When we begin to act in a spirit of disobedience, it will affect more than just us. It has repercussions far beyond our expectations.

~

Once you break the rank of submission, everything that is under you will begin to operate in the same spirit.

~

You shall observe this rite for an ordinance to you and to your sons forever.

—EXODUS 12:24

32

Taking the Anointing of Another

*S*oon after his disobedience of Saul's order, Jonathan started speaking against his father, against his leadership. He began to judge the instruction of his father, not being able to discern spiritually what was really happening inside of him. He was under his father's spirit of disobedience from the prince of the power of the air. He was being influenced by the spirit that challenges and disrespects authority.

Jonathan was under his father's spirit of disobedience from the prince of the power of the air.

When disobedience started to operate, this cord flowed through everything—starting when the supernatural anointing from Samuel, Saul's spiritual authority, was interrupted. Then disobedience ran down onto Saul (from the false authority, Satan), and that same spirit of arrogance and rebellion began to operate in Jonathan. Not long after, that same vile spirit started operating in others when they defiled themselves by sinning against God and eating not just blood, but even worse, fresh blood from raw meat. Each time sin multiplied.

Tragically, Saul found himself trying to correct something his own sin had given birth to. So he turned around and built his first altar unto the Lord (1 Sam. 14:35). In other words, Saul continued to operate under Samuel's transmitted mantle and anointing without developing an ultimate experience with God. He had become totally dependent on the fact that he was under Samuel's leadership, yet obviously felt he didn't have to pray or develop a personal relationship with God. He had received an impartation, but he was moving by association.

Think what would have happened if Jesus had stepped out from under His Father's authority on the cross. The glory would not have gone to God; it would have gone to Jesus—and Jesus wasn't the source of His own power. He had to remain under the power that His Father had transmitted to Him.

It is illegal for you to take an anointing that does not belong to you.

~

Tragically, Saul found himself trying to correct something his own sin had given birth to.

~

Then Jonathan said, My father has troubled the land. See how my eyes have brightened because I tasted a little of this honey. How much better if the men had eaten freely today of the spoil of their enemies which they found!

—1 Samuel 14:29–30

33

A Third Opportunity

*G*od still didn't forget His word to Saul. He sent the same man who had poured oil over him earlier—Samuel—back to him again. Samuel began to tell Saul all that God now said that he must do, instructing him to "go and smite Amalek and utterly destroy all they have" (1 Sam. 15:3).

Saul began to do what the Lord had commanded. He assembled the men and went forth to Amalek. There was going to be a great battle. But when it was all said and done, once again Saul failed to do *all* that God instructed him to do. Saul and his men spared Agag and kept the best sheep, oxen, fatlings, and lambs for themselves. They also kept anything else that seemed useful to them, destroying only undesirable or worthless possessions of the Amalekites.

Whenever there is disobedience in the leadership, it breeds disobedience in the people.

God was very angry with Saul because of his continued disobedience. "Then the word of the Lord came to Samuel, saying, I regret making Saul king, for he has turned back from following Me and has not performed My commands. And Samuel was grieved and angry [with Saul], and he cried to the Lord all night" (vv. 10–11).

There is nothing worse than having the anointing lifted off of your life because of disobedience—especially when you have received a rich impartation of an untainted anointing. It's a tragedy.

If you have been called under the hand of the Lord into leadership, you need to keep yourself in check. You need to let your mind go back to where God brought you from, to who and what you were before the Father caused this great transmitting of His power to be imparted into your life.

～

There is nothing worse than having the anointing lifted off of your life because of disobedience—especially when you have received a rich impartation of an untainted anointing.

～

Pride goes before destruction, and a haughty spirit before a fall.

—PROVERBS 16:18

34

Beware the Spirit of Perversion

*W*hen Samuel confronted Saul about his disobedience, Saul said, "Yes, I have obeyed the voice of the Lord and have gone the way which the Lord sent me, and have brought Agag king of Amalek and have utterly destroyed the Amalekites" (1 Sam. 15:20).

There is a powerful revelation in Saul's response. Saul didn't say, "Yea, I have obeyed the Lord." He said, "Yea, I have obeyed the voice of the Lord." Saul

Perversion is always laced with the truth.

did not have a relationship with God on a personal, spiritual level. His anointing had been imparted to him through the man of God, Samuel. Saul knew nothing about the prophetic; he knew nothing about prophesying, or what to do when the mighty Spirit of God came upon him. But he presumed to operate on that level, even though he knew it wasn't true. That's why he finished his sentence by saying, "…to sacrifice to the Lord *your* God" (v. 21, emphasis added).

When you "step over" into an anointing, and the mantle isn't yours, it becomes perversion. Once the spirit of perversion has entered in—meaning something that was ordained of God has begun to flow in an incorrect manner—it presents a reflection of the truth of God, but it actually yields the opposite result: it reverses His commands. Perversion is always laced with the truth. It is laced with *some* of the things God has said, but His words get turned around and twisted. Then, what God has spoken is brought outside of His order.

～

When you "step over" into an anointing, and the mantle isn't yours, it becomes perversion.

～

Obey your spiritual leaders and submit to them [continually recognizing their authority over you], for they are constantly keeping watch over your souls and guarding your spiritual welfare, as men who will have to render an account [of their trust].

—Hebrews 13:17

35

Being Attentive to God

*T*he enemy wants to make us believe that the Lord is more interested in what we sacrifice to Him—how we direct the choir, how good our message might be, everything involved with how we go about "doing good"—than He is in our obedience. We pervert the will of the Lord when we change it into a false glory, because the Lord isn't glorified when we walk in disobedience.

We pervert the will of the Lord when we change it into a false glory, because the Lord isn't glorified when we walk in disobedience.

Christians are constantly offering Him sacrifices and constantly telling God things like, "Well, I'm in Sunday school every week. I haven't missed a Sunday in ten years." "I'm the best choir director that anybody's ever seen...I have ten Grammys, nine Dove Awards, and five Stellar Awards. My record is at the top of the charts." But when it comes down to submitting to authority, submitting to the voice of God, and walking in obedience—respecting and acknowledging another man's authority, being yielded to the will of the one who has been called over us—they can't do that.

Be careful when you begin to operate in and transmit God's power, especially if the power within you is not properly submitted under spiritual authority. Unbridled power moves you into a desolate place, a place of poverty, lack, sickness, and disease. And worse, it can cost you the anointing God has imparted into your life; it can even impact your family. It is critical that as a child of your heavenly Father, you learn to submit to your spiritual fathers on earth.

~

God does not get the glory until we are walking in obedience to what He says.

~

There is need of only one or but a few things. Mary has chosen the good portion [that which is to her advantage], which shall not be taken away from her.

—LUKE 10:42

Section Six

The Generational Curse

36

Generational Repercussions

*T*he chain of events in Saul's life that led him to stepping out of spiritual authority into false authority can also be seen in the story of Uzziah. Once again, a young man got hit with the same cord of disobedience that had caused his natural father to disrespect authority. Hear me clearly. Disobedience runs from generation to generation, bringing curses upon each one. To understand the spiritual principles at work in the life of Uzziah, we will first take a closer look at the example of his father, Amaziah. Amaziah was only twenty-five years old when he began to reign, and he remained king in Jerusalem for twenty-nine years. The Word says that he "did right in the Lord's sight, but not with a perfect or blameless heart" (2 Chron. 25:2).

When leaders have a spirit of pride, it causes them to disobey the word of the Lord.

The Bible goes on to tell how Amaziah slew those who had killed his father but spared their children according to the Law of Moses (vv. 3–4). Then he assembled the men of Judah and Benjamin to lead them out for war against Edom without seeking the counsel of God. God reproved Amaziah by sending the prophet to him with this message: "O king, do not let all this army of Ephraimites of Israel go with you [of Judah], for the Lord is not with you" (v. 7).

We see this same principle in leadership today. There are leaders who have honored the prophets of old but who fail to honor the prophets among them whom God is sending to speak into their lives. When leaders have a spirit of pride, it causes them to disobey the word of the Lord, either because of the mightiness of their ministries or the strength of their talents and callings in God. There are always repercussions, which do not stop with the leader as a spiritual (or natural) father or mother. They will flow down from generation to generation, exactly as they did in Bible days.

~

Disobedience runs from generation to generation, bringing curses upon each one.

~

You shall not bow down yourself to them or serve them; for I the Lord your God am a jealous God, visiting the iniquity of the fathers upon the children to the third and fourth generation of those who hate Me, but showing mercy and steadfast love to a thousand generations of those who love Me and keep My commandments.

—EXODUS 20:5–6

37

Amaziah's Demise

*W*hen pride is in operation, leadership begins to act under the influence of the spirit of control. This is false authority. Why? These leaders are no longer letting the Spirit of God direct them. So they start commanding people to obey the dictates of their flesh, manipulating and coercing them to agree with and do things that aren't the will of the Father.

When we begin to worship what we have established—then we have made an idol of what we have conquered.

When this happens, God's people can no longer give back into those ministries according to the anointing they should have received from leadership. The spirit of control has silenced it. If these people stay steadfast in God, the Father will ultimately move them out of the way and bring judgment upon the false leadership.

If you are a leader, when you see issues running like cords throughout the church—attitudes, dispositions, character issues, and so on—then you need to check your own character. You need to check what you are birthing and imparting into your people, because they are giving back what they have received from your hands.

When Amaziah conquered the Edomites, the word of the Lord said he became so lifted up by what he had conquered that he brought their gods back and worshiped them. Amaziah began to boast about his victory, because he was no longer operating in the Spirit of the Lord—he was moving in his own might and power.

The prophet rebuked Amaziah, and Amaziah fell into pride. He threatened the prophet, and then turned around and disobeyed God again. Continue reading this story, and you will see that Amaziah was eventually overthrown and taken hostage (2 Chron. 25:15–25).

Amaziah was mighty, and his kingdom was strengthened until he became exalted in his own eyes. When he felt that he no longer needed to seek after God or to receive the word of the Lord, Amaziah's sins ultimately led to his death.

Authority is always accountable to authority.

I know that God has determined to destroy you, because you have done this and ignored my counsel.

—2 Chronicles 25:16

38

The Pattern Repeats

Uzziah, Amaziah's son, became king at age sixteen. Uzziah submitted himself under the tutelage of Zechariah, and as long as he sought the Lord, God prospered him. Unlike his father, he received his portion from the man of God. As a result, Uzziah became strong in the Lord. He was able to defeat the Philistines in their strongholds of Gath, Jabneh, and Ashdod, building cities for the Israelites right in the midst of these former Philistine strongholds. (See 2 Chronicles 26:6–10.) We learn that he became a very strong leader, and his fame spread all the way to Egypt. He strengthened the defenses in Jerusalem by building towers and hewing out cisterns. He had large herds of livestock and employed many farmers and vinedressers to tend the fertile fields.

The cord of disobedience from his father had been planted deep in Uzziah's soul—and he eventually repeated what he had seen in his natural father.

However, the cord of disobedience from his father had been planted deep in Uzziah's soul—and he eventually repeated what he had seen in his natural father. The Word tells us that he became proud, which led to his destruction. "He trespassed against the Lord his God, for he went into the temple of the Lord to burn incense on the altar of incense" (v. 16).

Do you see the pattern? At the beginning of his reign, King Uzziah was under spiritual authority. He had already established a way for his house to operate and the oil of the anointing to be released. But then the time came when he stepped over it, attempting to operate in a spiritual authority that was not his. When you become so great in your own eyes that you think you can operate in a spiritual office God has not anointed and appointed you for, you are putting yourself in a dangerous position. Uzziah was not a priest; he was a king. So he stepped out of his place in God and perverted God's divine order.

> When you become so great in your own eyes that you think you can operate in a spiritual office God has not anointed and appointed you for, you are putting yourself in a dangerous position.

> But when [King Uzziah] was strong, he became proud to his destruction; and he trespassed against the Lord his God.
> —2 CHRONICLES 26:16

39

God's Intended Purpose

*I*n 1 Chronicles 29:3–5, King David talks about the intended use of natural elements that would be used to build the temple, including stone, gold, silver, and bronze. Each element had a specific use. When the Lord commanded something to be formed from one piece of gold, it was beaten and shaped from one piece of gold. Oil was used for its intended purpose, gold for its purpose, and bronze for its purpose. Nothing was out of order. Everything remained in the place for which it was designed. Thus, when the temple was ultimately completed, it pleased the Father in its design.

> *Pride can creep in unnoticed and create a foothold for this foul spirit of disobedience.*

In just the same way, God has an intended purpose for each of His children. It is clear from the story about Uzziah that God intended for Uzziah simply to be the king. The Lord had not anointed him to be a priest. But, like the story of Saul we studied earlier, once again, strength bred pride, which led to disobedience. We must be careful when the Lord begins to strengthen us in ministry—when we start seeing the fruits of our labor. We must be careful when the Lord starts allowing our names to be spread abroad and we gain recognition, because strength can creep in unnoticed and create a foothold for this foul spirit of disobedience.

Uzziah trespassed against the Lord when he went in to the temple to burn incense on the altar of incense. Uzziah stepped over the spiritual authority God had appointed for him and became a diseased king under a false anointing. The same thing is happening in the church today. Leaders are still stepping out of their appointed spiritual authority and moving into false authority. Some are still preachers, but they are diseased. Others are still evangelists, but they have become diseased—they have stepped out of the will of the Lord by way of their own strength.

We must always remember to stay under the spiritual authority that God appoints for us and focus on *His* purpose for our lives.

~

God has an intended purpose for each of His children.

~

The Lord will perfect that which concerns me; Your mercy and loving-kindness, O Lord, endure forever—forsake not the works of Your own hands.

—PSALM 138:8

40

Operating in Human Strength

The apostle Paul understood that when you walk in human strength, you are usurping the authority of God. When Paul recounted his own life and the things that had happened to him, he made sure that he was not boasting of his own human strength. (See 2 Corinthians 12:5–9.)

Saul, Amaziah, and Uzziah began to boast of their own human strength. With Uzziah, however, not only did leprosy strike him because of his pride and disobedience, but he was also excluded from the house of the Lord. He didn't lose his kingdom, but he lost influence. This reveals another result of operating in human strength—we begin to feel as if we don't belong.

Uzziah did not lose his kingdom, but he lost influence.

For example, Sister Watermelon thinks, *I don't feel a witness that I'm still supposed to be in this church. People don't really accept my ministry. I feel like it's time for me to go, to change churches.* No! It is not time to change churches. Sister Watermelon has become leprous—because she stepped out from under the proper authority on her own counsel. She stepped over authority and usurped the instituted authority of God; therefore, she lost the spirit of humility. And where there is no humility, there is no brokenness. And without brokenness, Sister Watermelon was blinded and started heading toward destruction—because, as Proverbs 16:18 says, "Pride goes before destruction, and a haughty spirit before a fall."

Reflecting on Uzziah then, we can truly understand that in the midst of being corrected you can still be blinded because you can't see past your own strengths and accomplishments. Uzziah raged against God and the people of God, and he was a leper until the day he died. Sadly, even in death, he had no influence. Because he had become diseased, he had to be buried in the field of the kings outside of the royal tombs (2 Chron. 26:23).

Paul understood that when you walk in human strength, you are usurping the authority of God.

So for the sake of Christ, I am well pleased and take pleasure in infirmities, insults, hardships, persecutions, perplexities and distresses; for when I am weak [in human strength], then am I [truly] strong (able, powerful in divine strength).

—2 CORINTHIANS 12:10

41

History Repeats Itself

Whatever pattern we live by, we must understand we are not living for ourselves, but we are living to transfer a mantle to the next generation. Amaziah, as king in Jerusalem, stepped into false authority through pride. His son Uzziah assumed the throne and behaved the same way his father did. In 2 Chronicles 27 we meet Uzziah's son Jotham, who was a man of God.

In the fourth generation, the false anointing of disobedience comes into full bloom upon Ahaz.

Jotham broke the pattern of his forefathers. But the generational pattern still had an effect on his reign, because Jotham didn't get everything right. "He did right in the sight of the Lord, *to the extent of all that his father Uzziah had done*" (2 Chron. 27:2, emphasis added)—*not* beyond it. And the pattern of iniquity picked up again in the following generation. Jotham's son, Ahaz, began to rule when he was twenty years old. Unfortunately, he "did not do right in the sight of the Lord, like David his father [forefather]. But he walked in the ways of the kings of Israel and even made molten images for the Baals" (2 Chron. 28:1–2).

Now in the fourth generation, the false anointing of disobedience comes into full bloom upon Ahaz. He started sacrificing his own sons because he was a king under a false anointing. Hear me. A pastor, evangelist, or a teacher without an anointing will begin to destroy what is underneath them. False authorities destroy the people under their rule instead of birthing them out.

The cord of disobedience and false authority keeps getting worse from generation to generation. When you walk in a spirit of disobedience and are not submitted unto God, that spirit passes from one generation to the next, and the generation that follows becomes even more wicked. By the fourth generation of Amaziah, the entire nation of Israel had gone into captivity.

⁓

When you walk in a spirit of disobedience and are not submitted unto God, that spirit breeds itself down onto your sons.

⁓

The Lord…will by no means clear the guilty, visiting the iniquity of the fathers upon the children and the children's children, to the third and fourth generation.

—Exodus 34:6–7

42

Purification in the Church

$\mathcal{G}$od is crying out for sanctification and purification, not just for our sakes, but that the orderly flow of the anointing would not be hindered. If God's anointing is flowing out of our lives, generations further down the cord of Christendom will not be hindered. People beyond us will be saved and become completely submitted to God. If we can keep the orderly flow of the anointing from generation to generation, what a mighty church we will be!

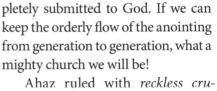

Your life and your anointing do not belong to you alone. You are accountable to the authority of God through the spiritual fathers who have gone before you.

Ahaz ruled with *reckless cruelty* against Judah and was faithless unto the Lord. So when he sent out to Assyria for help, the Bible says, "So Tilgath-pilneser king of Assyria came to him and distressed him without strengthening him" (2 Chron. 28:20). Why? If you are walking in disobedience, you do not receive help from others—nobody can help you except God. That is why you need to stay in purity before Him.

We are constantly challenged to walk consistently in faith toward God. If we do, we are promised in Psalm 84:11 that the Lord will walk with us: "For the Lord God is a Sun and Shield; the Lord bestows [present] grace and favor and [future] glory (honor, splendor, and heavenly bliss)! No good thing will He withhold from those who walk uprightly."

In this hour, we cannot afford to be self-willed. We cannot afford to insist upon our own way, because if we do, everything the Lord has lined up in our lives is going to be transferred to somebody else. Hear me. Your life and your anointing do not belong to you alone. You are accountable to the authority of God through the spiritual fathers who have gone before you. And remember, no matter what may have happened in the past, if you are willing and obedient unto God, you will eat the fat of the land. You don't have to stay under a curse!

~

If we can keep the orderly flow of the anointing from generation to generation, what a mighty church we will be!

~

Lean on, trust in, and be confident in the Lord with all your heart and mind and do not rely on your own insight or understanding. In all your ways know, recognize, and acknowledge Him, and He will direct and make straight and plain your paths.

—PROVERBS 3:5–6

43

Elisha's Double Portion

$\mathscr{E}$lisha gives us a positive example of the anointing and mantle of a spiritual father (Elijah) being passed down to his spiritual son (Elisha). Elijah walked with God. He went through a process of God leading him through different situations, and he reached the point where it was time to pass his mantle on to Elisha.

Elisha saw him taken away, and the Bible demonstrates that Elisha did indeed double the works that Elijah had done. But Elisha first had to submit himself to training. He submitted himself unto Elijah, walking with him daily for many years before he received Elijah's mantle.

In order to receive double, it has to flow down to you from someone else's measure.

Did you catch the revelation? In order to receive double, it has to flow down to you from someone else's measure. This is how greatness is birthed: the portion already within you balanced with the portion you inherit from your spiritual father. Then as God develops you, you begin to walk steadily in the integrity and discipline of His Word. And when you are walking in submission to the point that you are "buffeting your body" and consistently bringing your flesh under the divine will of God, another anointing is placed upon you…because of your level of obedience.

That is when you know that you are walking under the divine call and mantle God has placed over your life. The two have become one. Now, the anointing upon your life (and the things you should be able to accomplish in ministry) should be doubled. You should have the capacity to do double what your spiritual mentor has done, double that of the person with whom you have walked obediently in submission.

Yes, a godly anointing *multiplies.*

~

This is how greatness is birthed: the portion already within you balanced with the portion you inherit from your spiritual father.

~

Elijah said to Elisha, Ask what I shall do for you before I am taken from you. And Elisha said, I pray you, let a double portion of your spirit be upon me.

—2 Kings 2:9

44

Breaking the Curse…for Good

*A*maziah had received a false anointing from his father, Joash, who had followed after Ahaziah and Jehoram in their family line. That cord of disobedience kept flowing from generation to generation until Ahaz died.

Finally, after this fourth generation, Hezekiah was set into power. In the first month of the first year of his reign, Hezekiah opened the *doors* of the temple (which are symbolic of the *heart*) and repaired them. Then he made a declaration and charge to the *leadership*, exposing the work of the enemy and confessing the sins of the fathers that led to their captivity. Finally, he moved into a new day and started the *orderly flow of the anointing* by declaring a new covenant with God.

> *Hezekiah set the service of the Lord's house into order before he built his own house.*

Hezekiah reinforced the necessity for the priesthood to be attentive servants unto God, reminding them of their covenant responsibilities. Then the Levites sanctified themselves and carried out the unclean things from the temple. When the priests reported back to Hezekiah, he immediately reinstituted the temple sacrifices to atone for the sins of the nation. After this the song of the Lord came forth in worship until the burnt offering was complete—and then King Hezekiah and all who were with him bowed and worshiped (2 Chron. 29:21–29).

Hezekiah set the service of the Lord's house into order before he built his own house. And God, the eternal Father in heaven, was restored to His rightful place of glory and authority. So Hezekiah, the fifth from Amaziah, received grace to birth a new day for God's people—but notice, he did everything in "perfect" order. Everyone went back to his or her original positions in God, and the nation prospered.

The spirit of disobedience can be broken! The satanic cord can be severed. And you can find and stay in your place in God, no matter what you have been through in the past—because Jesus has gone before you. Turn your face to seek the Lord, and walk after the Spirit, praying acceptably unto God the Father. He will help you set your spiritual house in order and get aligned to receive a heavenly blessing.

~

The spirit of disobedience can be broken! The satanic cord can be severed.

~

So the service of the Lord's house was set in order.

—2 CHRONICLES 29:35

Section Seven

*T*he Power of Rebuke

45

A Loving Father Corrects His Children

Why must a spiritual leader rebuke? Rebuke keeps the body on course, and it ensures that you don't forfeit anything that God has for you. Correction from your spiritual father will keep you under spiritual authority and keep you from trusting in your own strength, thereby missing all that God has destined for you. Destiny is at stake. I am not just after "a few things" God has for me. I am after all of them. Therefore, I must embrace the power of rebuke.

If you are able to receive correction in your spirit, then you are at the place of wisdom.

Let me make this clear. When God puts you in the position to be rebuked, whether it's for something you have said, done, felt, or believed, He is announcing to you that He loves you. Many times, we doubt God's love for us. We expect Him to minister love to us the same way another person would—because we don't have a true concept of His divine nature. God doesn't express His love to us through presents, houses, cars, or goose bumps. He confirms His love when He corrects and rebukes us (Rev. 3:19).

If God is in the process of correcting your life, He has a portion for you, and He is getting your spirit ready. Why? If you are going to be used by Him in this last hour, it has to be done according to the method by which God instructed Zerubbabel—"…not by might, nor by power, but by my Spirit…says the Lord of hosts" (Zech. 4:6). By following this method you will remain open to correction, and you will impart life unto others. If you don't impart life, you will impart the spirit of error.

~

When God puts you in the position to be rebuked, He is announcing to you that He loves you.

~

The reverent and worshipful fear of the Lord brings instruction in Wisdom, and humility comes before honor.

—Proverbs 15:33

46

The Divine Order of Rebuke

*I*n the New Testament, the apostle Paul wrote a letter of correction to Titus. Paul wanted Titus to understand that he was not concerned with the gifts, callings, or talents of Titus. He was concerned with "cutting out" character in him.

Hebrews 13 lists some of the responsibilities of a person who is being corrected. We are instructed to "obey your spiritual leaders and submit to them [continually recognizing their authority over you], for they are constantly keeping watch over your souls and guarding your spiritual welfare, as men who will have to render an account [of their trust]. [Do your part to] let them do this with gladness and not with sighing and groaning, for that would not be profitable to you [either]" (v. 17).

> *Your spiritual leaders need to carve character in you to bring you to the level where you can handle the word you received.*

Why must you become submissive to the power of correction? Because it sends your spirit into training to learn how to renounce all ungodliness. Let me ask you this: how could you renounce ungodliness if you didn't know what ungodliness was? That's why we must receive correction. Our heavenly Father has to rebuke us (through His Word and our leaders) to expose ungodliness, so the next time it comes around, we can renounce it.

We must accept correction in order to stay clear of sin and claim our destiny.

～

Our heavenly Father has to rebuke us (through His Word and our leaders) to expose ungodliness, so the next time it comes around, we can renounce it.

～

He who heeds instruction and correction is [not only himself] in the way of life [but also] is a way of life for others. And he who neglects or refuses reproof [not only himself] goes astray [but also] causes to err and is a path toward ruin for others.

—PROVERBS 10:17

47

The Correction of Cain

When Cain and Abel brought sacrifices to God, Cain brought the fruit of the ground, but Abel paid his tithes. The Father was pleased with Abel's offering, and Cain got upset—so God had to rebuke him. I can just hear the Lord saying to Cain, "What's wrong with you? What's the matter with your faith? Why are you looking like that? Why are you acting crazy like this?"

God had to rebuke Cain about his actions so that he could learn to identify sin. God had to say, "If you don't do things the right way, with integrity, then your motive is incorrect—and that's called *sin*. But I

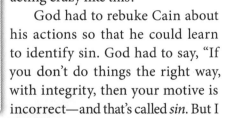

You can always tell when somebody hasn't received correction, because he or she will become disrespectful.

love you enough to tell you the truth and to correct you." Listen to me. Because of this, your spiritual father is more concerned with keeping sin from crouching at the door of your life than he is with your feelings.

Sometimes our spirits can get into a position where we believe we are more aware of God, and then we begin to think we are beyond correction. I see it happen all the time: "Well, I speak in tongues, so you can't correct me. I know the Lord. I can discern the way myself." It's all about, *"I, I, I.* What *I* can do now," instead of being about what God has already done!

Remember this: whatever God is correcting you about is beyond you. It is about your spiritual inheritance—what's coming through you to the next generation. It is about what's going to happen because of the choice you make to either accept or reject correction.

Anytime you are being instructed in the ways of God, and you refuse this instruction, you open your spirit to every diabolical act of the devil. You become vulnerable to his strategies. Then your spirit opens up to principalities under the devil's control, which begin to take control. Everything about you changes, and before you know it, you are sitting smack dab in the middle of the devil's camp.

~

Your spiritual father is more concerned with keeping sin from crouching at the door of your life than he is with your feelings.

~

If you do well, will you not be accepted? And if you do not do well, sin crouches at your door; its desire is for you, but you must master it.

—GENESIS 4:7

48

Rebellion Is Witchcraft

Oh, yes! When you reject correction, the spirit of witchcraft will try to take over—and no one on earth has to cast a spell or put something in your food. You have dropped something down into your own spirit man and put a hex on yourself. Rebellion will put you in the hands of every kind of witchcraft activity in the spirit realm. That is why God wants to break this evil spirit off of His people.

All of this happened because Cain brought the wrong seed to God. Something that small caused a divine domino effect.

If you are under a spirit of rebellion, it can tear your life apart—your finances, your children, and even your marriage. When you open yourself to a spirit of witchcraft, everything you touch will crumble. So if you are rebuked, be humble and examine your own spirit. Don't reject godly correction.

The little foxes destroy the vine. When God comes to you about something small, you had better say, "Yes, Lord." When you reject Him, you will fall to the level of deception and perversion. From there you fall to murder, rebellion, witch-craft, and poverty. Finally, the curse of being driven away from God's presence altogether will take effect—and that means losing your spiritual inheritance.

God's children aren't supposed to be without direction. When you belong to the Lord, He will lead you wherever He wants you to go.

Why would He throw you into a spirit of confusion? The journey we are on is leading us into the mysteries of God. The Father is saying, "If I can't get you to submit to the pastor, and I can't get you to submit to correction, then I can't take you any further. But if you don't submit, I cannot reveal my mysteries to you because you will become a loose cannon." God's process is to correct, train, and bless you now so that when you come into destiny, God doesn't have to correct and train you nearly as much.

~

God's process is to correct, train, and bless you now so that when you come into destiny, God doesn't have to correct and train you nearly as much.

~

In all your ways know, recognize, and acknowledge Him, and He will direct and make straight and plain your paths.

—Proverbs 3:6

49

The Power of Rebuke

$\mathcal{I}$f you stay submitted to spiritual authority, you can rise to a level where you are walking in the blessings of God because you understand His principles. Therefore, you don't offend God, because you hear His voice and obey. Are you ready to experience the fullness of His divine presence? Then let Him try your spirit through submitting to your spiritual father. Embrace the power of rebuke.

The order of God is for the body of Christ to function in unity—from the top down.

The order of God is for the body of Christ to function in unity—from the top down. This is how the fullness of His wisdom can be revealed. First Thessalonians 5:21 instructs us, "Test and prove all things [until you can recognize] what is good; [to that] hold fast." That's why we have qualifications for leadership, and that's also why a novice (an immature, inexperienced person) cannot serve in the ministry and have the capacity to watch over people's souls (Heb. 13:17).

Bearing this in mind, if you have rejected the correction of God, pray this prayer right now:

Break the spirit of rebellion out of me, God, and make me a servant. Create in me a clean heart. Renew a right spirit in me.

God wants to stop this spirit of rebellion by correcting you. He knows that some of the things with which you have been dealing aren't even about you—it was your mamma's sin or your daddy's rebellion. Maybe your great-granddaddy refused to be corrected, and now you are suffering a penalty. This is why it has to stop with you.

As a prophet of God, I speak it into the atmosphere for you to receive the birthing of Seth in your spirit. When Seth (the third son) was born to Adam and Eve, he then birthed the fourth generation, filled with men who began to turn their hearts back to God. As a result, prayer was restored, hearts were healed, and relationships were mended. Things started coming back into divine balance.

Oh, yes! There is power in rebuke.

~

Are you ready to experience the fullness of His divine presence? Then embrace the power of rebuke.

~

But test and prove all things [until you can recognize] what is good; [to that] hold fast.

—1 Thessalonians 5:21

Section Eight

The Absence of Correction

50

Purposes and Plans Are Established by Counsel

When you look at what God has demonstrated in the Scriptures, it becomes clear that receiving your spiritual inheritance means that God is going to discipline and prepare you to achieve greatness. God will make sure that you don't outrun, mishandle, or abuse the spiritual greatness He has put within you. Sometimes God calls us to do great things, and when we don't know it, we act foolishly. Like so many who have gone before us in the Bible, we mess everything up.

> God will never give you an assignment that doesn't require counsel.

When I was a little girl, my mother used to call me in from outside and make me sit down. I didn't know why she used to make me sit down, but on one occasion, about five minutes after I entered the house, somebody was hit by a baseball bat. On another occasion, ten minutes after she sat me down, somebody was run over by a car.

Now I understand that my mother could pick up in her spirit when a satanic force was about to hinder or try to destroy the call God had placed on my life. So she protected me from it.

If I had disobeyed my mother or snuck off and done things without her knowing where I was—it could have cost my life. There is a price to pay in the absence of authority, regardless of why the authority isn't there. Proverbs 20:18 says, "Purposes and plans are established by counsel."

Whatever the Father has for me, He will reveal His plans and purposes through the process of counsel. Let me say it to you another way. God will never give you an assignment that doesn't require counsel. If you plan to do something by yourself, then you can do that without asking anybody any questions. But if you want to recognize whether or not what you are about to accomplish is from the Lord, then one of the first signs is this: you will need some help with it.

~

If you are going to do something great for the Lord, then you are going to need His help and also the benefit of sound, spiritual counsel.

~

Purposes and plans are established by counsel.

—PROVERBS 20:18

51

The Mantle Dictates the Rules

*D*uring the Bible days of the prophets, there were laws that applied when somebody was being birthed in the prophetic. First of all, the Word of God must create something in you to establish who you are in the kingdom of God. Then rules must be established according to the mantle that is going to come upon you.

For example, the Holy Ghost gives a divine prophecy that you are going to preach all over the world. Your mamma isn't a preacher, your daddy isn't a preacher, and your granddaddy wasn't a preacher. Not even your great-granddaddy preached. As a matter of fact, there

What came upon Samson was a new thing.

are no preachers in your family, and nobody else in your family is saved but you. That's a creative anointing. That's when you know, without a doubt, that you are receiving the Father's portion, your spiritual inheritance.

However, it also means you have to "sit down" under godly teaching and training, because your portion came by revelation—you didn't inherit it from flesh and blood. It was created in the prophetic realm for you.

This principle can be illustrated in the life of Samson. Samson's mother was barren when the angel of the Lord told her that she was going to bear a son (Judg. 13:3). It was the Father's portion for her, but it came with conditions (vv. 4–5).

Samson's daddy might not have been strong, and his grandmamma probably didn't lift weights. What came upon Samson was a new thing. Because the mantle was a creative new thing, the Lord established the rules to which Samson must submit to inherit the full portion of the destiny God had for him.

∿

The Word of God must create something in you to establish who you are in the kingdom of God.

∿

For behold, you shall become pregnant and bear a son. No razor shall come upon his head, for the child shall be a Nazirite to God from birth, and he shall begin to deliver Israel out of the hands of the Philistines.

—JUDGES 13:5

52

Samson's Disobedient Heart

*S*amson wasn't blessed with the spiritual inheritance simply because God liked his mamma. There was a divine purpose for his strength. God has a purpose for what He is raising you up to do, and He will accomplish that purpose. Samson was told that he wasn't to touch anything unclean. He was instructed not to cut his hair. He was a *Nazirite*, which means separated and set apart.

The purpose of the anointing God placed upon Samson was to deal with Israel's enemy.

One day, Samson went to Timnah and saw a Philistine girl. Samson returned to his parents and said, "I like that girl; get her for me." (See Judges 14:3–4.)

Then Samson was attacked by a young lion (v. 5). Even though Samson was able to kill that lion effortlessly, the Bible states that "*he did not tell his father or mother what he had done*" (v. 6, emphasis added).

As I read these verses, God kept bringing to my attention the fact that Samson didn't tell his parents about killing the lion. The Lord spoke something to me, whispering in my spirit this: "Had

Samson told his mother and father that he had killed a lion, it would have given them an opportunity to say, 'Don't misuse the strength that God has given you. It's not for your own purposes.'"

Then, while Samson was traveling home, he passed the carcass of the lion and found a swarm of bees and honey. Remember that Samson wasn't supposed to touch or eat anything unclean—but he desired it, so he ate the honey, anyway. I knew right there that Samson was headed for trouble.

Samson knew he was a Nazirite; therefore, he was to remain separated. But when he came into knowledge and recognized the power of God on his life, he started making the wrong decisions. I can just hear him thinking, *Now, I can eat anything I want. I can go where I want to go.*

Believers do the same thing today. We get a little knowledge of our portion and think, *I don't have to go to church. I don't have to be there every service. I don't have to come on time. I don't have to do what they tell me to do, because I'm mature. That's for the others who are still babies.* Wrong!

~

God has a purpose for what He is raising you up to do, and He will accomplish that purpose.

~

And Samson said to his father, Get her for me, for she is all right in my eyes.

—JUDGES 14:3

53

The Age of Accountability

After Samson ate the honey, his parents stopped challenging him. He scooped honey, and not only did he eat it, he gave some to his parents. Samson defiled them! You see, when you are a parent in the Spirit, if you do not stay on guard in the Spirit, your own child can defile you.

Notice the way Samson talked to his parents, "Get her for me" (Judg. 14:3). Samson saw that woman and started trying to rule everybody! But his soon-to-be wife would slip from his grasp. Fear was driving her to figure out his secret. Verses 12–20 tell the rest of the story. Samson gave a riddle, and she exposed what it meant. Afterward the Spirit of the Lord came upon Samson, and he killed thirty men of that city and took their clothes for spoil. He was angry because they threatened his wife and got the secret to the riddle.

God can use you even when you are wrong…but be careful…you could be working for the kingdom while on your way to hell.

Samson had taken those first steps out from under the covering of spiritual authority. Then things continued to get worse for him. In anger, he killed those thirty men and took their clothes. Then he became angry with his wife also, and he left her to return back to live with his parents.

Samson's parents should have told him, "Go back and get your wife." Instead, he lived with his parents for four months. When the time for harvest came, he became full of lust and wanted sex with his wife. So he went back to Timnah with a gift for her and demanded to sleep with his wife (Judg. 15:1–2).

But her father replied, "I thought you didn't want my daughter, so I gave her away."

What did Samson do? He went and caught three hundred foxes, twisted their tails together, lit them with fire, and then sent them into the enemy's camp, scorching the harvest (vv. 4–5). At this point, Samson had great power, but he was out of control. He had an anointing—he had received a portion from God—but there was an absence of correction. Nobody was there to chastise him and channel that anointing.

~

Samson had great power, but he was out of control. He had an anointing—he had received a portion from God— but there was an absence of correction.

~

And the Spirit of the Lord came upon him, and he went down to Ashkelon and slew thirty men of them.

—JUDGES 14:19

54

A Proven Leader

*S*amson was called and prepared to be a leader, but the qualifications were not evident in his life. He had power, but he also had a bad temper. He had an anointing, but he lacked self-control. Samson wasn't disciplined or temperate. He wasn't longsuffering—he was just strong. And he justified his actions by saying, "This time shall I be blameless as regards the Philistines, though I do them evil" (Judg. 15:3).

> *People who are trying to operate in an anointing without correction will always justify their wrongdoings.*

In other words, he was saying, "I'm not to blame for what I'm about to do." People who are trying to operate in an anointing without correction will always justify their wrongdoings. They will blame it on "what God has said" and what He told them to do. They will justify their own sin by exposing the acts of the other person. They will blame what they did on everybody else.

There are many people in the body of Christ today who have moved out of God's direct call because they are going by what their own spirits told them to do.

Rebuke is absolutely necessary for people who carry strength, for those who know the direction of God in their lives. Samson justified to himself that he was only paying the enemy back for what they had done to him. But that revealed a flaw—because a true anointing doesn't retaliate. An anointing that is under the correction and submission of authority never responds by using it to get back at anybody. Scripture tells us that after Samson retaliated against the Philistines, the enemy sought him out, and he picked up the jawbone of an ass and killed a thousand men (Judg. 15:9–17).

Here was a judge of Israel, a man separated to God from birth and raised up in strength and power. But because he had no one speaking truth into his life through rebuke, his actions grew progressively more disobedient.

~

Rebuke is absolutely necessary for people who carry strength, for those who know the direction of God in their lives.

~

And Samson said of them, This time shall I be blameless as regards the Philistines, though I do them evil.

—JUDGES 15:3

55

The Absence of Correction

In Judges 16, Samson traveled to Gaza and slept with a prostitute while there. Guess what? He was still God's anointed even though he was sleeping with a prostitute. He still had strength. He was still powerful. But he didn't have anybody who was bold enough to say, "You can't do that; you're a Nazirite. Do you remember what God told you? You don't have any business sleeping with a prostitute. You're set apart; you're God's anointed."

Samson was a mighty man of God, but his flesh got out of control. From the beginning, he didn't submit to the leading of God.

By that time, everybody was interested in his gifts and talents. Everybody was impressed with how anointed he was. Hear me. That is why you have to pull back when people start giving you compliments, "Oh, you're anointed…God's going to use you." I personally don't want to hear that, because when I get through being used, I want to be saved! When I get through preaching, I don't want to be shipwrecked.

The Bible says a good name is rather to be desired than riches (Prov. 22:1). Samson desired a Philistine, and he fell deeper and deeper into defilement. It happened because there was an absence of correction in his life. When people are not under submission, they often start sneaking around and conniving. When you refuse to accept correction and to submit your life under the proper authority, the devil confronts you with a demon that has been designed to match your strength.

Samson was a mighty man of God, but his flesh got out of control. That's what drove him to the Philistine girl. Samson never said, "I've prayed about it, and God showed me that this girl is going to minister to my life. She's going to help me fulfill my goal to become a judge over all Israel." No! He said, "Get her for me…I like her." From the beginning, he didn't submit to the leading of God.

~

When you refuse to accept correction and to submit your life under the proper authority, the devil confronts you with a demon that has been designed to match your strength.

~

A good name is rather to be chosen than great riches.
—PROVERBS 22:1

56

A Father's Anointing Covers Your Vision

*S*amson became a mighty man with an anointing, but he did not have a covering anointing to guide his life. Are you getting this? There was a spiritual inheritance laid up for him by God—yet on every level, when he avoided correction, his sin multiplied. Finally Samson fell in love with Delilah, and a lying spirit jumped to the surface. When you reject correction, all kinds of spirits jump on you!

> *Samson lost his ability to seek God in every situation.*

Samson lied to Delilah three times and broke free. But finally, he was trapped by his sin. This is a powerful revelation. When the Philistines burst in, Samson jumped up as he always did, thinking, *I have the power*—but he didn't have it. People do the same thing today—they jump up and preach even though they don't have the anointing anymore. People sing all the right notes in praise, but they aren't anointed as they used to be. What's worse, there are people saying, "Amen," to preachers based upon the anointing they used to recognize in those preachers. They shout and dance from the residue of what they used to have.

The saddest thing about what happened to Samson is that he lost his eyesight. He lost spiritual discernment. Slowly but surely, he lost his ability to seek God in every situation. Therefore, he couldn't discern the enemy's devices, and he ended up being led around by a servant.

Near the end of his life, Samson wanted God to strengthen him because he had lost his eyesight. In the realm of the Spirit, this represents insight. The presence of correction brings insight to properly release the portion God has for you. But the absence of rebuke will pull you out of submission and obedience. In the process, you will lose your insight while you are messing around in the devil's camp.

~

The absence of rebuke will pull you out of submission and obedience.

~

O Lord God, [earnestly] remember me, I pray You, and strengthen me, I pray You, only this once, O God, and let me have one vengeance upon the Philistines for both my eyes.

—JUDGES 16:28

57

Eli's Disaster

*W*hy is rebuke necessary? Let's take a look at Eli, the high priest in Israel when the word of the Lord was shut up in the land. (See 1 Samuel 1–3.) Eli knew his sons were sleeping with women in the temple, yet he waited to correct them (1 Sam. 2:22–25). Because of this, God wouldn't talk to him. How could God speak to Eli about a nation when He couldn't even speak to him about his sons?

Rebuke…godly correction…is part of God's preparation of His children for their spiritual inheritance.

Eli had been in the tabernacle all of his life; he was raised up as a priest. Then he blessed a woman who was crying out for a child, and three years later, Samuel was brought to the tabernacle. That child, Samuel, didn't know anything. His mother dedicated him to the Lord and left him in his Father's house. God chose Samuel to receive his spiritual inheritance. In the third chapter of 1 Samuel, Samuel heard a voice calling his name (vv. 1–10).

The fact that he was dedicated to the temple means that Samuel was also under a Nazirite's anointing—he was set apart. Anyone who has been set apart for the Master's use can hear God talking. Eli wasn't a good leader, but Samuel stayed there because that was where he had been placed. He maintained his position and stayed where God told him to stay.

Rebuke…godly correction…is part of God's preparation of His children for their spiritual inheritance. Rebuke comes your way because you are strong. It is a trick of the devil to come to you and tell you that you can't make it because you are so depressed. Why do you think he's pressing in on you like this? It is because he is trying to break your strength. Therefore, if your leader doesn't correct you, then the power and might of who you are in your intellect would lead you into an illegal zone in the Spirit.

~

Remember that God still uses His anointed even when they become disobedient.

~

Touch not My anointed, and do My prophets no harm.
—1 CHRONICLES 16:22

58

The Sin of Achan

hy must our leaders rebuke? Look at the story of Achan, who stole the thing God had devoted to destruction and then lied about it. One man stopped the whole church! When Ai rose up in Joshua 7 and defeated the army of Israel, only a few people were able to chase three thousand Israelites away from their city gates. (See Joshua 7:1–5.)

> *There are more Christians today than ever, and still, we don't have authentic power over the devil. Why? Because there is sin in the camp.*

Joshua and the elders of Israel came to the Lord in deep desperation (vv. 6–10). God's response to Joshua was merely to say, "Get up! Why do you lie thus upon your face?" (v. 10). There are some things you pray about and others that you step up to the plate on. God told Joshua, "This isn't the time to pray. This is the time to confront, rebuke, and instruct." Then He said, "Israel has sinned; *they* have transgressed My covenant…" (v. 11, emphasis added). He didn't indicate that it was one man who had transgressed His covenant—it was an entire nation.

They were a company going to battle; therefore, in the eyes of God, "I" became "US."

Remember this. When you choose to fall into sexual sin, and then you go to church pretending and don't repent—*you* just got *us* in trouble. When you play an instrument in the body of Christ, and your hands aren't clean and your heart isn't right, *you* are messing *us* up. Verse 12 indicates that because of one man's sin, "the Israelites could not stand before their enemies."

Why do we need correction? Why is there power in rebuke? We need correction because a whole nation could rise and fall if just one person doesn't learn how to stay in submission to God. A whole church could suffer if one person hides from correction. And most importantly, the spiritual inheritance reserved especially for you is awaiting your full obedience. Will you embrace the greatness God has put within you?

‿

A whole church could suffer if one person hides from correction.

‿

They have transgressed My covenant which I commanded them. They have taken some of the things devoted [for destruction]; they have stolen, and lied, and put them among their own baggage.

—Joshua 7:11

Section Nine

The Spirit of Truth

59

The Word of Truth

The reality is that God can give us a portion and bring His work to completion—but if we don't submit our lives to divine instruction, rebuke, and correction, we will end up shipwrecked in our faith. It's not enough to have a great call on your life; it's not enough just to know there is a spiritual inheritance for you. Your call must be directed, confirmed, and proven by the word of Truth—that is how you know you belong to God.

How can you be in the presence of almighty God, read His Word every day, and still desire to live in sin?

You have to know for sure that you got saved *for real*. My Bible tells me this: "Old things are passed away; behold, all things are become new" (2 Cor. 5:17, KJV). How can you be in the presence of almighty God, read His Word every day, and still desire to live in sin? The Holy Spirit (the Spirit of Truth), who lives inside of you, won't allow it—He will send conviction until you change. When Jesus washes your sins away, He gives you a new heart and then starts transforming your mind. You should never be the same!

Even when we find ourselves in times of correction from God, we are advised to remember that "the Lord corrects and disciplines everyone whom He loves, and He punishes, even scourges, every son whom He accepts and welcomes to His heart and cherishes" (Heb. 12:6). We have been adopted into the family of God. Therefore, "You must submit to and endure [correction] for discipline; God is dealing with you as with sons. For what son is there whom his father does not [thus] train and correct and discipline?" (v. 7).

~

Your call must be directed, confirmed, and proven by the word of Truth—that is how you know you belong to God.

~

The sheep that are My own hear and are listening to My voice; and I know them, and they follow Me.

—John 10:27

60

Watch Out for "Bigger and Better"

*J*udas walked with Jesus every day, hearing the Word and seeing miracles, but he was double-minded in all his ways. Even though he traveled with Jesus, I doubt that he spent much time in His presence—and that's when temptation gets the best of you. Judas was tired and dissatisfied, and he thought he saw something "bigger and better" on the horizon. He betrayed the Lord while trying to create a "portion" for himself, and then he died without receiving it. (See John 13:1–30; Matthew 27:3–5.)

While you are talking about getting to your next level in God, He's watching...closely.

Too many people are waiting for God to lay something "heavy" on them. They have their own ideas about what the Father should do, but they are blind to their own shortcomings. Let me tell you something. If you can't handle the weight of the attack of the enemy, you will never be able to handle the weight of the anointing for anyone else—because the anointing is much heavier than anything the devil could even put on you.

While you are talking about getting to your next level in God, He's watching…closely. When you are going through a fiery trial, do you still come to church? Do you still praise Him, or do you just sit in the pew with your lips cocked to the side? If you are coming through some things in your finances, do you withhold your tithe? If your kids drove you crazy this week, did you let it affect your relationship with God? Are rivers of living water flowing out of your spirit?

~

Are rivers of living water flowing out of your spirit?

~

And they have no real root in themselves, and so they endure for a little while; then when trouble or persecution arises on account of the Word, they immediately are offended (become displeased, indignant, resentful) and they stumble and fall away.

—MARK 4:17

61

Spiritual Racehorses

$\mathscr{E}$verybody wants to win a race, especially when we see a reward. You have to decide who you are based on the truth. Ask yourself, *Am I like a field horse or a racehorse?* Let's look at the process. From what I was told, horse trainers go someplace like Australia and find wild horses—with strong muscles and teeth, beautiful structures, and shining coats—galloping through the hills. They are beautiful and free, but they lack purpose and direction.

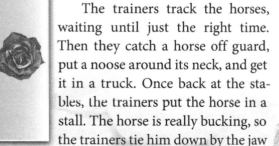

If you are going to reach your destiny, if you are going to receive and activate your spiritual inheritance, you have to be willing to accept rebuke.

The trainers track the horses, waiting until just the right time. Then they catch a horse off guard, put a noose around its neck, and get it in a truck. Once back at the stables, the trainers put the horse in a stall. The horse is really bucking, so the trainers tie him down by the jaw with the ropes close to the railing. He has to be trained to stay in the stall—because during a race, he must stay there until the door is opened. The horse must learn how to begin.

The hardest part comes when they clamp a bit in the horse's mouth. The horse literally goes crazy, because he doesn't like anything controlling his mouth. The trainer, on the other hand, is trying to help the horse understand, "If you let me control your mouth, then when you're running a race, you can be guided around anything that gets in the way. You can get past your struggle, past your opponent, and beyond anything that's trying to hold you captive. I can teach you how to win the prize."

Listen to me. If you are going to reach your destiny, if you are going to receive and activate your spiritual inheritance, you have to be willing to accept rebuke. When you are corrected, be humble and honest with yourself. Don't get upset when God uses somebody to bring correction in your life. You are not like a field horse. You are a thoroughbred from a royal family line. God is driving you to win.

God is training you because He sees greatness in your spirit.

～

You are a thoroughbred from a royal family line. God is driving you to win.

～

Do you know that in a race all the runners compete, but [only] one receives the prize? So run [your race] that you may lay hold [of the prize] and make it yours.

—1 Corinthians 9:24

62

God Wants Your Participation

*Y*ou won't receive your spiritual inheritance just because you are having a high time in the Spirit. Your life isn't going to change just because you are shouting and dancing. No! God is calling for your participation, because for too long, the body of Christ has been sitting back saying, "Prophesy over me" and God is saying, "No! I've already done My part."

When your life is full of integrity and you put your spirit in the posture to be trained, heaven will open.

If you want to see heaven opened...if you want your divine portion...you don't need somebody to prophesy over you. When your life is full of integrity and you put your spirit in the posture to be trained, heaven will open.

So please understand me when I say that leadership can't be concerned about your feelings. Think about this: the clothes you are wearing right now have been cut according to a pattern. The Father created a pattern for you (from those who have gone before you). Now He is making sure to cut you the right way so He can duplicate a pattern of righteousness in your children, friends, and others in your circle of influence. Again, it's not just about you. Do you want God to activate spiritual destiny in your life? Then submit to the training, preparation, and correction that prepare you for that destiny. Don't be satisfied with junk food, cookies, candy, and prophecies; only hunger *and thirst* for the presence of God in your life—learn to embrace the Spirit of Truth.

~

Do you want God to activate spiritual destiny in your life? Then submit to the training, preparation, and correction that prepare you for that destiny.

~

Then He said to him, I assure you, most solemnly I tell you all, you shall see heaven opened, and the angels of God ascending and descending upon the Son of Man!

—JOHN 1:51

Section Ten

The Making of a Son

63

Adopted Into the Royal Family

$\mathscr{M}$ultimillionaires don't just give inheritances to people they have just met. Inheritances are earned by way of DNA (that is, blood relationship), adoption, or close relationship. In order to receive an inheritance, you have to be born or adopted into a family and then live respectably within that family.

When you have been born again and adopted into the Royal Family, you must embrace the truth. You now possess the DNA of your heavenly Father, and there will be some requirements for bearing His name. Hear me. In order to carry the name of Jesus and to be associated with the kingdom of heaven, you must adopt a lifestyle of submission and obedience to your Father's will.

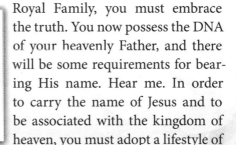

Submission in the course of a relationship between a spiritual parent and a son or daughter is very powerful.

This requirement also applies to the spiritual leaders God has appointed to stand in His stead and speak on His behalf. A leader cannot speak on behalf of the Father and His Word if he or she has no relationship with Him. Without proper submission and obedience to God, a spiritual leader cannot hear the Lord—which means many simply hear their own intellects. When this happens, the people God has ordained to sit under their tutelage (as spiritual sons and daughters) aren't fed properly. Starving for true spiritual knowledge, they can become unruly in the Spirit, because they are being pacified by intellectual stimulation when divine direction is needed.

Submission in the course of a relationship between a spiritual parent and a son or daughter is very powerful. Because we only want to embrace the good in our spiritual leaders, many people in the body of Christ are thrown for a loop when their leaders are unfaithful or sinful. We must learn to recognize that the bonds of spiritual relationship are strengthened by the process of walking through both good—and *bad*—with that person. That is the only way authentic relationships can be proven.

~

In order to carry the name of Jesus and to be associated with the kingdom of heaven, you must adopt a lifestyle of submission and obedience to your Father's will.

~

For all who are led by the Spirit of God are sons of God.

—ROMANS 8:14

64

A Man After God's Own Heart

God said that David was a man after His own heart. Why? Because David was a man of truth. David yielded himself completely to God, and when he messed up, he admitted his sins and got it right. Through every experience, David learned how to examine his own heart and submit himself to God. Whether he was facing a lion, bear, Goliath, or King Saul, David exemplified what being a son or daughter of the kingdom is all about.

We must begin to see leadership as people who are standing in the stead of God and learn to follow their spiritual direction.

Spiritual authority and leadership must be defined. The role of a spiritual son or daughter in relationship with God and with his or her spiritual parent needs to be defined. Unless the body of Christ begins to understand this role, we will continue to hinder the move of the Holy Spirit in the earth. We must begin to see leadership as people who are standing in the stead of God and learn to follow their spiritual direction.

SECTION TEN

Samuel had two natural sons who did not walk in his ways, and they served badly as judges over Israel. Therefore the people told Samuel they wanted a king (1 Sam. 8:4–7). In obedience to God, he anointed Saul as king. But Saul did not walk in his ways, either, so God took the kingdom from him.

But remember that Samuel had honored his spiritual father, Eli. When King Saul rejected the Lord and Samuel's spiritual mentorship, Samuel remained obedient to God, wiped his tears, got up, and went to Bethlehem where he would anoint David as the next king of Israel. Prophetically, the number four represents the supernatural manifestation of God, so by the time Samuel reached David, something powerful was going to be released.

Samuel was the "spiritual father" of the nation, so when he anointed David, an orderly anointing from the heavenly Father was poured out upon David's life. (See 1 Samuel 16.) Once again, Samuel's obedience to God was absolute. Because of that anointing, proper spiritual protocol was poured out onto David.

Spiritual authority and leadership must be defined.

Then Samuel told the people the manner of the kingdom [defining the position of the king in relation to God and to the people], and wrote it in a book and laid it up before the Lord.

—1 SAMUEL 10:25

65

Catch the Vision of the Father

*D*avid not only received the anointing to become king, but he also received the supernatural ability to become a true son. But Saul didn't know how to be a father. He hadn't been anointed for it. God is your Father in heaven. When He gives you a father in the earthly realm (your pastor), you must remain a son or daughter—even if your leader hasn't yet received the anointing to be a father or mother.

> *Once you tear the authority of the person that is over you in the Lord, the same authority is automatically torn from you.*

Saul had disobeyed God, and because of his disobedience, he was suffering the penalty when David came into the camp. David entered Saul's camp walking in obedience to God, and as a result David's life demonstrated the power of his anointing. This distressed Saul, for it was a vivid reminder to him of the anointing he once had in his life. In an incident recorded in 1 Samuel 15, God gave Saul a visual picture of the devastating result of his disobedience.

Samuel wore a prayer shawl (a *tallit*) with four corners, each with five knots in the tassel that extended from it. These five knots represented the five ways and names of God. In 1 Samuel 15, Samuel confronted Saul with his disobedience, indicating that he would not return with Saul to the temple and allow Saul to worship God. This greatly distressed Saul, and as Samuel turned to leave, Saul grabbed the hem of Samuel's mantle, tearing off a corner of it (v. 27).

Recognizing the visual picture this act of disobedience would give to Saul, Samuel said to him, "The Lord has torn the kingdom of Israel from you this day and has given it to a neighbor of yours who is better than you" (v. 28).

Grasp the significance of this lesson for us today. Once you (the person who is submitted under authority), by your disobedience, tear the authority of the person that is over you in the Lord, the same authority is automatically torn from you. This is a spiritual principle that you must never forget.

~

When God gives you a father in the earthly realm (your pastor), you must remain a son or daughter—even if your leader hasn't yet received the anointing to be a father or mother.

~

The Lord has torn the kingdom of Israel from you this day and has given it to a neighbor of yours who is better than you.

—1 SAMUEL 15:28

The Prophetic Death Sentence

When Saul's daughter Michal fell in love with David, Saul recognized an opportunity to set David up to be killed. (See 1 Samuel 18.) He sent orders for David to bring him one hundred foreskins from the Philistine army as a prerequisite to marrying Michal. This was virtually impossible to do. Yet, because David had already received an anointing to walk into his next realm with God, he came back with two hundred Philistine foreskins, won Saul's daughter in marriage, and dealt prophetically with the enemy's assignment against Israel—past, present, and future—all at the same time.

> *David was under proper spiritual alignment and had a contrite heart, so God could place an anointing upon him to take down the spirit of the Philistines.*

After Saul gave Michal to David in marriage, he became David's enemy continually. But the Bible says that David behaved himself wisely. (See 1 Samuel 18:27–30.) If you read the whole story of David and Saul, you will find that at least two or three times David is described as behaving and handling himself respectfully when Saul came against him.

Regardless of what Saul did, David never got out of order. He learned how to remain under his anointing—because he understood his purpose. He also understood that he was called to minister to Saul. Whenever the evil spirit of the Lord would start overtaking Saul, David would start ministering (1 Sam. 16:15–23).

Some people are anointed to sing in the choir; others are anointed to play the keyboard or guitar. Some are anointed to usher or direct the choir. Still others are anointed to put together hospitality. When you see your spiritual leaders going through something, that's your opportunity to get in your anointing— because that is what ministers to them. Remember your "measure of faith"? It is part of how God makes you into a son or daughter of the kingdom. Staying in your lane is important.

> When we submit to proper spiritual alignment, strongholds start coming down.

The priest said, The sword of Goliath the Philistine, whom you slew in the Valley of Elah, see, it is here wrapped in a cloth behind the ephod; if you will take that, do so, for there is no other here. And David said, There is none like that; give it to me.

—1 Samuel 21:9

67

Interceding for Your Spiritual Leaders

One day, David and his men were in a place called En-gedi, resting in the darkness of a deep cave (1 Sam. 24). Saul came into that same cave, not knowing that David and his men were in the cave's "innermost recesses" (v. 3). David watched as Saul relieved himself, which represents a state of vulnerability or weakness because his private parts were exposed.

> Whatever God allows you to see about your leadership, that's what takes you from being a baby saint and a "bench man" to an intercessor.

Let's look at this prophetically. David saw the waste, the filth that was coming out of Saul's body. I say "filth" because urine and bile are bacteria. They are the "trash" that gets purged from our flesh. David went up behind Saul and cut his robe. And when he came out of the cave, he yelled back at Saul, saying, "Saul, let me show you this. I have the corner of your robe."

We need to learn from this. Whatever God allows you to see about your leadership, that's what takes you from being a baby saint and a "bench man" to an intercessor—because everybody in the church can't see it. When God starts allowing you to see certain things, it's because your leaders really need your prayers! They need the intercession of a mature believer.

God proved David so that whatever happened in the kingdom, David would always desire to do what was right in His eyes. David endured the process of being made into a true spiritual son. Therefore, God could trust David with His kingdom...because He could trust him with His king.

God is saying today, "I can trust you with the kingdom if I can trust you with My king. I can trust you to cover My kingdom if I can trust you to cover my king." Are you ready to become a true son or daughter of the kingdom and receive your spiritual inheritance?

~

God is saying today, "I can trust you with the kingdom if I can trust you with My king. I can trust you to cover My kingdom if I can trust you to cover My king."

~

And Saul knew David's voice and said, Is this your voice, my son David?

—1 SAMUEL 26:17

Section Eleven

The Seduction of Jezebel

68

It's About Relationships

*I*n order to understand the process by which Jezebel is exposed and dismantled, we must understand the power of what having a lineage really means. Why? Because everything that God is dealing with you about individually isn't just about you. It's bigger than you are. It's bigger than me.

God is calling the body of Christ to be unified and purified.

The Father's portion is about generations. It's about relationships. This is why Christ came as a son from a Father into the womb of a mother. God is about *family*.

Why is this important? If you don't know where the root of a spirit comes from, you will be frustrated for the rest of your life, fighting the symptoms. And I promise you that the body of Christ has been guilty of fighting Ahab and Jezebel and not really getting to the root from which they came. In order for God to deliver the church from the attacks of Jezebel and Ahab, we must be able to establish them as symptoms—not the strong man.

The reason why Jezebel attacks and wins is because those who preach the gospel have not presented the full knowledge of where this spirit came from. This is why Hosea 4:6 says we are destroyed for a lack of knowledge. Yet this will not be our fate any longer.

Why must we embrace a corporate call? Because our adversary, the devil, has already launched a counterattack on the corporate level—the spirit of Jezebel. This spirit may attach itself to individuals, but its goal is to achieve a much bigger purpose. The spirit of Jezebel intends to frustrate the plans of our heavenly Father, to wreak havoc in the church, and to stop His purposes. And as we have discovered, a false anointing also has a lineage. Therefore, anyone who doesn't live in submission and obedience to God can easily come under its influence.

~

Our adversary, the devil, has already launched a counterattack on the corporate level—the spirit of Jezebel.

~

I in them and You in Me, in order that they may become one and perfectly united.

—JOHN 17:23

69

The Lineage of Ahab

*K*ing Ahab, Jezebel's husband, was the product of an evil lineage that started when God took the kingdom of Israel from Solomon, David's son, at which time the prophet Ahijah named Jeroboam as king.

During his reign, Jeroboam had a constant power struggle against Rehoboam, Solomon's son. In fear of losing his kingdom, Jeroboam manipulated the people of God and perverted God's prophetic plan by leading the entire nation into idolatry (1 Kings 12:25–33). As a result, the Lord set Himself to cut off the house of Jeroboam from the face of the earth (1 Kings 13:33–34).

Jeroboam's story is a classic example of receiving the Father's portion—and a warning about crossing over into false authority.

Jeroboam's counterfeit anointing went beyond his generations, affecting his son Nadab and Nadab's successors to the throne—Baasha, his son Elah, Zimri, and Ahab's father, Omri, who "did evil in the eyes of the Lord, even worse than all who were before him. He walked in all the ways of Jeroboam"

(1 Kings 16:25–26). Then Ahab was born, and sin multiplied. During Ahab's twenty-two-year reign, "Ahab did more to provoke the Lord, the God of Israel, to anger than all the kings of Israel before him" (v. 33).

Take some time and read 1 Kings 11–16 for yourself. You will discover that when you open up your spirit to disobedience by refusing instruction and avoiding correction, then you become prey to a false anointing. And this spirit isn't just after you. It wants the spiritual inheritance that our Father has set aside for you—in order to take down His kingdom.

～

When you open up your spirit to disobedience by refusing instruction and avoiding correction, then you become prey to a false anointing.

～

Moreover, the Lord will raise up for Himself a king over Israel who shall cut off the house of Jeroboam this day.

—1 Kings 14:14

70

The Lineage of Jezebel

*W*ebster's dictionary defines the word *Jezebel* as "an impudent, shameless, morally unrestrained woman." Impudent means, "marked by contemptuous or cocky boldness or disregard for others." This vile spirit doesn't regard anybody. It is unteachable; it cannot be led—it is sure it already knows the way.

Jezebel is the prop—the frame—not the real enemy. She was raised in evil, therefore giving her a passion to operate in perversion (meaning taking God's version and God's way and twisting them until they fulfilled her own evil desires).

*Jezebel is the prop—
the frame—
not the
real enemy.*

The last three letters of her name, Jez*ebel*, are not spelled exactly like *Baal*, but it has been made clear that Jezebel was birthed from an idolatrous lineage when Ahab married her. When studying in the *International Standard Bible Encyclopedia,* I found that the names *Baal* and *Bel* could be used interchangeably.

Something stirred within me when I read these words: "I gave her time to repent, but she has no desire to repent of her immorality" (Rev. 2:21). *If Jezebel was given an opportunity to repent, then she must not have been the chief spirit.* Why? Because the devil can't ever repent and be saved!

This confirmed to me that there is a ruling spirit that controls Jezebel. For years, the church has pointed the finger and declared, "It's Jezebel...it's the Jezebel spirit." We've lived under the illusion that Jezebel is controlling our churches, when, in fact, Jezebel is the deception. *She's not the real thing.* She's the decoy that the devil has been using to shift our focus and to deceive us. The real culprit behind Jezebel has been hidden for centuries.

~

We've lived under the illusion that Jezebel is controlling our churches, when, in fact, Jezebel is the deception. *She's not the real thing.*

~

And Ahab son of Omri did evil in the sight of the Lord above all before him.... He took for a wife Jezebel daughter of Ethbaal king of the Sidonians, and served Baal and worshiped him.... And Ahab made an Asherah [idolatrous symbol of the goddess Asherah].

—1 KINGS 16:30–33

71

The Origin of Baal

*F*irst Kings 16:33 says that Ahab did more to provoke the Lord than all the kings of Israel that were before him. What really provoked the Lord wasn't simply the fact that Ahab married Jezebel, because he was already evil. What provoked the Lord is that he erected a statue (an idolatrous image) called an *Asherah*.

Hear me! The church is not fighting against a mere woman! We must pull down the *stronghold*...the "proud and lofty thing" that controls her.

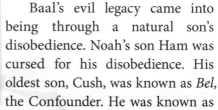

Hear me! The church is not fighting against a mere woman!

Baal's evil legacy came into being through a natural son's disobedience. Noah's son Ham was cursed for his disobedience. His oldest son, Cush, was known as *Bel*, the Confounder. He was known as the god of confusion because he founded Babylon. Do you notice that the name *B-e-l* has the same spelling as the end of the name Jeze*bel*? Every time you see the word *Bel* or *Baal*, it is a suggestion that there is confusion in the midst.

Cush's son Nimrod was the first man to war against his neighbors. The *Chumash* states: "Nimrod ensnared men with his words and incited them to *rebel* against God." Do you see the word *rebel*? This is why rebellion is as the sin of witchcraft (1 Sam. 15:23).

Nimrod married his mother, Semiramis, and they became known in Egypt as Isis and Osiris. The pagans worshiped both the mother and the son as gods—which introduced the worship of Baal and his female counterpart, Ashtoreth. This was the birthing of perversion, the further establishment of self-will when man stopped seeking after the will of God and started seeking his own.

~

Every time you see the word *Bel* or *Baal*, it is a suggestion that there is confusion in the midst.

~

For rebellion is as the sin of witchcraft.

—1 Samuel 15:23

72

Get to the Root of the Problem

When my editor, Paula Bryant, and I were working on my author review copy of the manuscript that I had received back from the publisher, we came to the realization that Jezebel was not the primary spirit—*she was the form that was being used by a much greater force.*

Some time later, a young woman walked over to me and said, "Prophetess Bynum, six months ago I went to a bookstore, and this book was in a basket of books that were for sale." And she told me, "When you got through preaching on Sunday about the spirit of Ashtaroth, God led me to give you this book. He told me that it would confirm some things to you."

The poles were intended to deny and denounce the root that would come out of Jesse, which was Jesus Christ.

Everything that was in this book, God had given us through our studies! As recorded in 1 Kings 16:30–34, temples of Baal and Ashtoreth were built together. This encouraged the Israelites to worship these false gods among the "groves" of trees that were cultivated in the temple. An *Asherah* was comprised of sacred poles that were placed in the grove near Baal's altar. God revealed to me that these poles or trees being grown in the ground of the temple were intended to deny and denounce the root that would come out of Jesse, which was Jesus Christ. I can see why God was provoked to anger at the disobedience of Ahab.

~

Jezebel was not the primary spirit—she was the form that was being used by a much greater force.

~

And he shall be like a tree firmly planted [and tended] by the streams of water, ready to bring forth its fruit in its season; its leaf also shall not fade or wither; and everything he does shall prosper [and come to maturity].

—PSALM 1:3

73

The Roots of Jezebel

*R*ecently I was watching a television special about Hawaii. One segment of the show explained how in one group of fish, the *Wrasse,* several females cohabited with one male. The male was bigger and stronger than all of the females, so it was his job to defend them against predators.

When the male dies, however, the largest, most aggressive female literally undergoes a sex change and becomes a male!*

This deceptive spirit tries to copycat the anointing and to pervert what the word of the Lord has established.

For some reason, this information wouldn't leave my spirit. Now I know why. One of Ashtaroth's most ancient forms comes under the name of *Atar-gatis,* a woman with the tail of a fish! In other locations where she was worshiped, the dove was her sacred symbol. Yet another form of Ashtaroth, the moon goddess, was symbolized by the horns of a cow. Can you see the roots of Jezebel? Do you see

---

*Information obtained from a telephone interview with Delbeek, Waikiki Aquarium, 3/7/04.

how she works? This deceptive spirit changes shape and form, always trying to copycat the anointing and to pervert what the word of the Lord has established.

We see this illustrated in the revelation in the story of Ahab and Jezebel. In order for Jezebel to be released into her full, false anointing, her husband had to relinquish his authority. Ahab did that when he served and worshiped Baal and then built an altar for Baal and an Asherah. Through the abdicating of his own authority, he allowed the spirit of Jezebel to be loosed!

This spirit can only reign in places where spiritual authority has been voluntarily relinquished. The spirit of Jezebel cannot rule where she hasn't been given authority. We cannot be passive about the things of God! If we know the Word of God and fail to do what we know, we can become a prey to this spirit. Hear me. This is real. We must walk boldly into our spiritual inheritance!

~

We cannot be passive about the things of God!

~

But be doers of the Word [obey the message], and not merely listeners to it, betraying yourselves [into deception by reasoning contrary to the Truth].

—JAMES 1:22

74

The Mantle of Elijah

*W*hen King Saul set David up to be killed by the Philistines, David came back with two hundred foreskins—a double portion of what Saul had asked for. The Philistines worshiped Ashtaroth in her warlike form. So David's victory in order to marry Michal was also a prophetic seed for Elijah's victory on Mount Carmel in 1 Kings 18.

You can't get the Father's portion in a hurry.

David remained obedient to his anointing throughout his life. But his son Solomon did not. As a result, God split Solomon's kingdom for his disobedience and gave ten tribes to Jeroboam (1 Kings 11:29–39). Then years later, when Ahab (the seventh king from Jeroboam) was in power and his sin multiplied, God sent Elijah to take the spirit of Ashtaroth down.

There is an important lesson to be learned through this history of David's anointing down through the line of kings to wicked King Ahab. David had obtained a double portion of foreskins (200) for King Saul. Generations later, Elijah defeated twice as many enemies as David had when he defeated 450 prophets of Baal. This double-portion anointing then transferred down to Elijah's spiritual son, Elisha, for he received a double portion of Elijah's anointing.

When Elijah was coming to the end of his assignment, and the Lord was going to take him from the earth, Elisha asked for a double portion of Elijah's spirit (1 Kings 19:9). Twenty-five years had passed from the moment when Elijah threw his mantle upon Elisha until this time. You can't get the Father's portion in a hurry. Elisha was proven to be a son over the course of time.

Elisha did receive a double portion from the Lord—performing twice as many miracles because the anointing of his father, Elijah, had multiplied. I believe that Elijah's anointing started operating in Elisha's life the moment Elijah tossed him the mantle in 1 Kings 19:19. It was definitely a spiritual impartation.

~

Elisha did receive a double portion from the Lord—he performed twice as many miracles because the anointing of his father, Elijah, had multiplied.

~

So Elijah left there and found Elisha son of Shaphat, whose plowing was being done with twelve yoke of oxen, and he drove the twelfth. Elijah crossed over to him and cast his mantle upon him.

—1 KINGS 19:19

75

Elijah's Prophetic Word

*K*ing Ahab and his wife, Jezebel, ruled Israel together, using the devil's false anointing to create an environment of wickedness and sin throughout all Israel. When it was time for this wicked dynasty to end, King Ahab was the first to die. His death came as the result of his wicked attempt to steal the property—and spiritual inheritance—of Naboth, who owned a vineyard coveted by the king (1 Kings 21:1–4).

When Jezebel talked to her husband, he told her what had happened. This released her to operate under the covering of his false anointing.

When Jezebel talked to her husband, he told her what had happened when Naboth refused to sell him the vineyard. This released her to operate under the covering of his false anointing. She devised a plan, wrote letters in her husband's name, and executed the order to have Naboth killed. When she returned and told Ahab that Naboth was dead, "he arose to go down to the vineyard of Naboth the Jezreelite to take possession of it" (v. 16).

God didn't waste any time either. God sent Elijah to confront Ahab with his sin. Elijah prophesied that Ahab would share the same destruction he had inflicted upon Naboth (vv. 17–19). Elijah also prophesied the death of Jezebel (vv. 23–25).

In the next chapter of 1 Kings, though Ahab had repented in sackcloth and ashes, he rejected the word of the Lord. His death sentence was carried out when he went to battle against Syria with Jehoshaphat, king of Judah.

Ahab died facing his enemies. When the battle ended, they carried his body to Samaria and buried him. But I want you to see this: they washed the blood out of Ahab's chariot "... by the pool of Samaria, where harlots bathed, and the dogs licked up his blood, as the Lord had predicted" (1 Kings 22:38). Ahab despised correction and lost a generation.

~

Ahab despised correction and lost a generation.

~

And he answered, I have found you, because you have sold yourself to do evil in the sight of the Lord.

—1 Kings 21:20

76

Jehu's Divine Assignment

*J*ehu (Jehoshaphat's son) was anointed to be king over Israel after Ahab's death and given divine instruction to "strike down the house of Ahab" (2 Kings 9:7). God promised to "make the house of Ahab like the house of Jeroboam son of Nebat and like the house of Baasha son of Ahijah. And the dogs shall eat Jezebel in the portion of Jezreel, and none shall bury her" (vv. 8–10).

This portion of Scripture shows us why the spirit of Jezebel hates order. Jehu wasn't anointed because he had fasted, prayed, and went on a consecration with some friends. He was anointed because God was executing His plan. The orders were being fulfilled! God had already given Elijah the mantle to bring down the prophets of Baal. Through Elijah, He had granted a double-portion anointing unto Elisha—and then Elisha sent a prophetic word to Jehu (the son of Jehoshaphat, a righteous king from David's lineage).

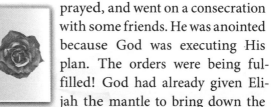

Jehu was anointed because God was executing His plan.

God's divine order would finally take down the spirit of Jezebel at its roots…the false anointing that had passed down the line through her husband, Ahab. Yes, spiritual alignment will always get her in the end—because it is a corporate anointing.

～

God's divine order would finally take down the spirit of Jezebel at its roots.

～

Thus says the Lord, the God of Israel: I have anointed you king over the people of the Lord, even over Israel. You shall strike down the house of Ahab your master, that I may avenge the blood of My servants the prophets and of all the servants of the Lord [who have died] at the hands of Jezebel.

—2 Kings 9:6–7

77

We Must Become a Company Coming

*J*ehu put into action the Lord's plan to destroy Jezebel. When a watchman on the tower in Jezreel saw Jehu and his army approaching the city, he ran to the king to tell him that he saw a company of soldiers coming (2 Kings 9:14–17).

How is the church going to destroy Jezebel? How are we going to dismantle that spirit? We have to become "a company coming." There is a time when we must respond as spiritual racehorses, stepping up into destiny under the leadership of our spiritual fathers. But in a horse race, only one can win the prize. When it is time for us to become "a company coming," we must respond like warhorses—

> When symptoms keep cropping up, it indicates that you haven't captured the strong man.

charging toward the enemy as one. That is how the church leaders in the Book of Acts ministered unto the Lord in order to receive His direction. They stopped talking, started seeking, and kept obeying. And they did it in unity. That gave no place to the devil.

As the people of God, we have to come against Jezebel as a company.

When leadership is functioning in divine order, we will chase the spirit of Jezebel and the evil spirits in partnership with the devil down until their power is destroyed.

~

Divine order must flow through the channel of leadership.

~

When Joram saw Jehu, he said, Is it peace, Jehu? And he answered, How can peace exist as long as the fornications of your mother Jezebel and her witchcrafts are so many?

—2 KINGS 9:22

78

Jezebel Tries to Change Her Image

*S*omething interesting happened when Jehu arrived at Jezreel. "Now when Jehu came to Jezreel, Jezebel heard of it, and she painted her eyes and beautified her head and looked out of [an upper] window" (2 Kings 9:30).

God revealed to me that when it's time for Jezebel to die, like a chameleon, her spirit tries to become beautiful. She sud-

When it's time for Jezebel to die, like a chameleon, her spirit tries to become beautiful.

denly starts acting sweet and kind: "Oh, I love you." "God bless you." But God will say, "I still see you, Jezebel. You're the same demon, even though you painted your eyes and beautified yourself." Listen to me. By receiving Jesus Christ, we have become the sons and the daughters of God with a prophetic lineage. Therefore, we have spiritual vision. We can see past the surface and expose the enemy.

Jehu recognized Jezebel in her disguise and called to those watching from the windows, "Who is on my side?" (v. 32). There were two or three eunuchs looking on who threw

Jezebel down to Jehu, splattering some of her blood on the wall and on the horses. Jehu drove over her with his chariot, ending her life (v. 33).

Now hear me on this. A eunuch is physically sterile, so he can't reproduce. The spirit of Jezebel was not going to be able to pervert the generations of those eunuchs. But neither would they produce any children who could move into destiny. There may be times when you feel as though your spiritual father is keeping you from moving into destiny. When your leader is dealing with you in correction and "sits you down" from ministry, don't think you will never be able to produce. He or she is not trying to hurt you or to hold you back. God can still use you against the enemy. If you take on the mind of a servant (like Christ) and stay submitted to spiritual authority, you can be a part of bringing Jezebel down.

~

By receiving Jesus Christ, we can see past the surface and expose the enemy.

~

Now when Jehu came to Jezreel, Jezebel heard of it, and she painted her eyes and beautified her head and looked out of [an upper] window.

—2 KINGS 9:30

79

Jezebel Must Fall

*M*any believers have been too busy fighting over seats and titles in the church and trying to get in the pastor's favor. You see, a lot of people are coming into the church, but there are only a handful of servants. Many have taken on the spirit of Jezebel—they have become spiritual bloodsuckers. This foul spirit must fall. The Holy Spirit is calling the body to "grow up." We must come to maturity so that we can be part of a mighty company that carries out the vision God has given to our spiritual parents.

We must be part of a mighty company that carries out the vision God has given to our spiritual parents.

In order to reach spiritual maturity, we must cry out to God and say, "God, my heart isn't right before You. Help me get to the place in You where I'm walking, talking, and living right." Take inventory of your motives. Are you trying to build your own ministry?

You will never defeat the spirit of Jezebel from your life or from the body of Christ with ungodly motivations. It must be the Lord who is building the house. It must be the Lord who is leading you to step into destiny.

Jezebel must fall. Your personal vision must support the vision of the man and woman of God. God is building His church, and our purpose—no matter what kind of portion He has given us—is to build His kingdom. The church isn't about seats or activities or personalities. It's not about *you*; it's not about *me*—it's much bigger than any one person. The Father's portion is about souls. Activate your measure of faith in the Lord, because He has already finished His Father's business and can help you to finish your course.

~

> The church isn't about seats or activities or personalities—it's much bigger than any one person. The Father's portion is about souls.

~

> And he said, Throw her down! So they threw her down, and some of her blood splattered on the wall and on the horses, and he drove over her.
>
> —2 KINGS 9:33

80

A New Day, a New Anointing

*J*ezebel has to go. She can't stay in power because the church is moving forward into our divine destiny. A powerful anointing is flowing in the church. It's our time in the Father's prophetic plan. Jesus is coming soon, so God is getting His house in order. The "portion" He has set aside for you is being united with others to fulfill His purpose.

> Jezebel can't stay in power because the church is moving forward into our divine destiny.

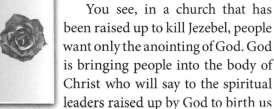

You see, in a church that has been raised up to kill Jezebel, people want only the anointing of God. God is bringing people into the body of Christ who will say to the spiritual leaders raised up by God to birth us into destiny, "I'm here to serve you. Even if you don't give me a dime, I'm going down with the ship."

Break Jezebel's subtle seduction. Ask your pastor, "How can I be of help? Where do you need me to work?" Find time in your schedule to help to build the house of God. Receive your spiritual inheritance from the Father, and activate it. It's our time, and everybody's gifts and abilities are needed. When you get under the flow of an orderly anointing, God will bless your life more than you could ask or think.

Jesus has already outlined and fulfilled the process that will set us free. As we *believe*, *trust*, and *rely* on Him, we will be more than able to do it.

~

Jesus has already outlined and fulfilled the process that will set us free. As we believe, trust, and rely on Him, we will be more than able to do it.

~

Whoever wishes to be great among you must be your servant, and whoever desires to be first among you must be your slave—just as the Son of Man came not to be waited on but to serve, and to give His life as a ransom for many [the price paid to set them free].

—MATTHEW 20:26–28

Section Twelve

Babylon's Fall

81

The Fall of Babylon

$\mathscr{I}$n the end, Babylon is going to fall—God Himself will judge her. (See Revelation 17:3–6.) When Babylon goes down, every demon spirit will live there. "She is fallen! Mighty Babylon is fallen! She has become a resort and dwelling place for demons, a dungeon haunted by every loathsome spirit, an abode for every filthy and detestable bird" (Rev. 18:2).

Like Baal, Ashtaroth takes on different forms and manifestations according to strongholds that are present in the hearts and minds of the people. For example, if a person is an alcoholic, Ashtaroth can be operating. At the same time, if another person is caught up in homosexuality, her "sex change" manifestation is in operation. This means whatever you "love" can open the door to her demonic influence.

> Believers are chasing demon spirits and binding "symptoms," but our real enemy is Babylon— their demonic stronghold.

This really hit me. So many Christians have been running around binding demons, but in reality we are just dealing with the symptoms! Each demon has a specific manifestation (lust, pride, and so on)—but from these verses in Revelation we learn that Ashtaroth (Babylon) is at the core of each manifestation. This passage tells us that in the end all demons are going back "home"...*to her.* Babylon is their *dwelling place.* Babylon gets her power from the beast, and demons are released from Babylon.

On every level, this spirit has tried to copycat the order of the Lord. But in the end, just like the beast on which she rides, Babylon will be consumed with fire. Everything this deceptive spirit gained when the people of God willingly gave up their place of authority is going to be stripped away from her for good.

~

In the end, Babylon is going to fall. God Himself will judge her.

~

And he shouted with a mighty voice, She is fallen! Mighty Babylon is fallen! She has become a resort and dwelling place for demons, a dungeon haunted by every loathsome spirit, an abode for every filthy and detestable bird.

—REVELATION 18:2

82

We Are the True Bride of Christ

After Babylon falls, the saints rise in splendor and majesty! This is why the "false bride," Babylon, controls the "merchandising" of all the fine things of the earth: purple, scarlet, linens, and every type of costly good. The counterfeit bride, the female companion of the beast, Babylon puts her merchandise on parade, showboating against the church. This

The true inheritance is righteousness, our Father's character. It is "dazzling and white."

is also why her thirst for wealth, power, and influence is never satisfied. It doesn't rightfully belong to her...IT IS NOT HER INHERITANCE! Revelation 19:3–8 tells us that the *true inheritance* is righteousness, our Father's character. It is "dazzling and white." Babylon will never have any part of it, so she wars against the church by parading the things she loves.

Babylon is glorified in prosperity. Therefore, saints must be careful, because prosperity is readily given through her false anointing. That's why it is critical in this hour to stay in spiritual alignment. We must be certain our prosperity is of the Lord. Hear me. *We can't judge by blessings.* Babylon controls the marketing (merchandising)—which isn't spiritual prosperity. True prosperity—our spiritual inheritance—comes by the favor of the Lord, which includes financial rewards. And when the Lord blesses His sons and daughters, there's no sorrow added with it (Prov. 10:22).

Those who are under Babylon's spell are arrogant and cocky about their prosperity. This is a sign. You will be able to see ugly things in their spirits—because they are under the false spiritual alignment of Baal and Ashtaroth. But the fruit of the Spirit will be evident in the lives of those who stay under godly alignment, along with the blessings of God (Gal. 5:22–23).

~

It is time to rise up and take what rightfully belongs to us!

~

Let us celebrate and ascribe to Him glory and honor, for the marriage of the Lamb [at last] has come.

—REVELATION 19:7

Section Thirteen

The Real Authority

83

Jesus Is the Real Authority

*I*f we live according to the Word in our true spiritual inheritance, Jezebel can't rule. That is why we must learn to say *yes* to God and have hearts that constantly seek after His will. We will have real authority in Jesus Christ if we live in obedience to the Holy Spirit. As we learn from the example of Jesus when He walked on earth, yielding is the only way to obtain and maintain our dominion over the enemy. Yielding keeps us in a posture of true sonship "in Christ," where we have an expected inheritance.

Once and for all, Jesus dealt with the spirit of Jezebel— through a woman who dared to be obedient.

When Jesus was about to meet the woman at the well of Samaria, He said to His disciples that it was necessary for Him to go through Samaria (John 4:4–18). Why was it necessary? All of Israel knew that Samaria was a cursed land. Jesus stopped at the well outside the city where He encountered the Samaritan woman. This woman had gone through five husbands and was with another man who also wasn't her husband. That's when God said, "Go back and count…"

Seven wicked kings ruled in Jeroboam's dynasty after God split Solomon's kingdom in 1 Kings 11 (see verses 29–39): Jeroboam, Nadab, Baasha, Elah, Zimri, Omri, and Ahab. All were part of an evil, natural legacy, so none were true "fathers" of Israel. Death and destruction came to each one as the spirit of Jeroboam moved down the line—that is, until Jesus showed up. That day at the well, Jesus came as the "seventh" man (the righteous Seed). He canceled the wicked lineage over the Samaritan woman's life and "perfected" God's prophetic plan.

Isn't it just like God to send His Son to reverse the curse in that place? Once and for all, Jesus dealt with the spirit of Jezebel—through a woman who dared to be obedient. He canceled an evil spiritual legacy over her life, the lives of the Samaritans, and the entire world all at one time!

～

If you have opened the door through disobedience and let Jezebel in, rebuking the devil isn't going to change a thing!

～

So be subject to God. Resist the devil [stand firm against him], and he will flee from you.

—JAMES 4:7

84

God Maintains His Power

God foreknew that the powers of darkness would fight to keep His eternal plan from coming to pass. But since He is the real authority, no power in heaven, on earth, or under the earth can resist Him. (See Psalm 14:2–3.)

God looked out over the world He had created and was grieved at what He saw. He was grieved because man had eaten of the tree of the knowledge of good and evil. He was grieved that He had tried so many different ways to introduce His law and ways to the people, and every time they failed.

When you are in Christ, Jezebel—or any other demon spirit—does not stand a chance.

When God brought the Israelites out of slavery in Egypt, He had to speak by feeding them quail and manna, leading them with a cloud by day and a pillar of fire by night. (See Exodus 16:12–15; 13:21–22.) Joshua and Caleb were the only ones of their generation to reach their destiny, because they were able to recognize and embrace their Father's vision. From the beginning of mankind, God has been saying, "You must follow Me. You must follow My ways. You must do things My way." There is no other way to reach destiny.

To receive our full inheritance as sons and daughters of the kingdom, we have to come through Jesus Christ—the real authority—the prime example of sonship. Before He created time, God knew how to maintain His authority. He knew that He would look down upon creation and be grieved at the state of man, so He made provision in His Word to do something about it.

When you are in Christ, Jezebel—or any other demon spirit—does not stand a chance. The grief our heavenly Father experienced can be transformed into divine pleasure through the obedience of Christ.

~

When our heavenly Father foresaw mankind's need for a Redeemer, Jesus said, "Father, here I am…send Me."

~

It was the will of the Lord to bruise Him; He has put Him to grief and made Him sick. When You and He make His life an offering for sin [and He has risen from the dead, in time to come], He shall see His [spiritual] offspring. He shall prolong His days, and the will and pleasure of the Lord shall prosper in His hand.

—ISAIAH 53:10

85

Jesus, Our Ultimate Example

*J*esus became the ultimate example of sonship because He went through the process. He started out with the Father in heavenly places and was sent out from the Father to earth. He was sent; He didn't just go. Jesus was sent out from heaven to fulfill the vision and will of the Father in the natural realm. That's why it didn't matter how hard it was for Him to pay the price for our sins. Because He was sent, Jesus could say, "Nevertheless…"

When everything you know is being tested and tried, will you still stand and say, "Nevertheless, I will do my Father's will"?

All power was put in Jesus' hands because He "gave all" by going through the process of the Father in proper order—He was born of a virgin, raised in Bethlehem, baptized by John in the Jordan River, tempted for forty days and nights…I could go on and on. So let me ask this question: If God is for you (and He is), who can be against you? If God is for you, can you embrace submission and obedience? Can you trust God to order your steps and give you counsel through a spiritual father on earth? Can you trust Him in everything, even though you can't see what may happen tomorrow?

That is why I said earlier that a spiritual father sees who you are to become. When a leader recognizes the calling of God on someone's life, there's something about that person's presence that satisfies the leader's spiritual intuition. Why? He knows this son or daughter will go through a process in the physical realm, even if he or she has already committed to assisting with the vision. There will always be a process.

Now, are you more convinced than ever that you are ready to become a true son or daughter of the kingdom and receive your spiritual inheritance?

～

All power was put in Jesus' hands because He "gave all" by going through the process of the Father in proper order.

～

All authority (all power of rule) in heaven and on earth has been given to Me.

—Matthew 28:18

Section Fourteen

Our True Inheritance

86

Sacred Pearls

To become a son or daughter of the kingdom, you must embrace your Father's character and do what pleases Him. Earlier we took a look at the prodigal son (Luke 15:11–32). He thought the physical part of his inheritance was all his father had to offer. But after leaving his father's house and losing everything—he discovered that physical rewards soon perish.

If you open the "gate" of your life to the enemy, he will trample everything under his feet and then try to take you out.

The father was still wealthy and powerful, but the son lost the benefit of his good name…*because he failed to recognize its value.* Proverbs 22:1 says, "A good name is rather to be chosen than great riches, and loving favor rather than silver and gold." The prodigal son disrespected his father's name, and in doing so, he despised his godly lineage—so he lost his place of authority. He became poor, like any other man without an inheritance. And he ended up feeding pigs just to survive.

Jesus said, "Do not give that which is holy (the sacred thing) to the dogs, and do not throw your pearls before hogs, lest they trample upon them with their feet and turn and tear you in pieces" (Matt. 7:6). Your "pearls" are sacred. Let's see why. In Matthew 13:45–46, a pearl describes the kingdom. In Revelation 21:21, the holy city of Jerusalem (that will come down from heaven) is described as having twelve gates, each made of a solid pearl…and the "gates of Hades" can't prevail against these heavenly gates—because they are built on a revelation of who the Father really is.

Gates represent power. They also symbolize how you can give entrance to either good or evil. If you truly know your Father, you have the authority to do His works. So if you don't, what happens? The enemy can't take what you don't willingly give up.

If you open the "gate" of your life to the enemy, he will trample everything under his feet and then try to take you out.

~

Your "pearls" are sacred.

~

Do not give that which is holy (the sacred thing) to the dogs, and do not throw your pearls before hogs, lest they trample upon them with their feet and turn and tear you in pieces.

—MATTHEW 7:6

87

Habitual Obedience

*J*esus said, "You are the salt of the earth, but if salt has lost its taste (its strength, its quality), how can its saltiness be restored? It is not good for anything any longer but to be thrown out and trodden underfoot by men" (Matt. 5:13). Salt not only enhances the natural flavor of food, but also it is a preservative. Do you see the revelation? Your "kingdom" lineage protects

Your true inheritance is in your Father's house.

you from the enemy and enables you to serve beyond your natural abilities—because that is what you inherit from your heavenly Father. His character is supernatural.

Jesus recognized the importance of stepping beyond the natural into the supernatural character of His Father. When His parents discovered that He had remained in Jerusalem, sitting among the teachers and rabbis in the temple, His response to His parents was this: "How is it that you had to look for Me? Did you not see and know that it is necessary [as a duty] for Me to be in My Father's house and [occupied] about My Father's business?"

(Luke 2:49). As a result of His desire to step beyond the natural, He "increased in wisdom (in broad and full understanding) and in stature and years, and in favor with God and man" (v. 52).

Even as a child, Jesus knew that being in His Father's house and serving the Father's vision was His first priority. But His parents didn't comprehend what He was saying—and many Christians today are in the same place. We don't understand the importance of submitting to a vision and helping to bring it to pass. Jesus was "habitually obedient" to His heavenly and earthly authorities. Therefore, His Father's character grew within Him. He gained wisdom and stature, and He had favor with God and man.

What about you? Are you serving in the house of your spiritual father or living to serve your own needs? Your true inheritance is in your Father's house. It's the strength of your Father's character.

～

Jesus was "habitually obedient" to His heavenly and earthly authorities. Therefore, His Father's character grew within Him.

～

You are the salt of the earth, but if salt has lost its taste (its strength, its quality), how can its saltiness be restored? It is not good for anything any longer but to be thrown out and trodden underfoot by men.

—Matthew 5:13

88

The Seven Eyes of God

*I*n Zechariah we read about the seven eyes of God (Zech. 3:7–10). God has been speaking strongly to my spirit about the *seven eyes*, because this is how He is rebuilding His kingdom. During Zechariah's ministry, the Israelites had just come out of slavery in Babylon and returned to Jerusalem to rebuild the temple—so God set the *seven eyes* before the high priest. He imparted His vision and the manifestations of His character to leadership, because Israel had a great work to complete. It had to be accomplished by His might and power.

> *Unless we remain submitted to God and to those in positions of divine authority, the anointing to break every yoke and reestablish our spiritual foundation will be hindered.*

Seven is the perfect number of God, so the seven eyes of the Father have been given to the Son—and His vision is perfect. Nothing is hidden from His eyes. This is how every part of the church will become spotless, white, and without blemish. The "might" and "power" of the flesh will fail. Only that which is birthed by the Holy Spirit (the sevenfold radiations of God) will fulfill the plan of the Lord in this final hour. The day of "human wonders" is over. God is doing things His way.

The Holy Spirit is moving mightily in the earth; therefore, we must not hinder what He is doing through our disobedience. Submission is critical. Unless we remain submitted to God and to those in positions of divine authority, the anointing to break every yoke and reestablish our spiritual foundation will be hindered.

Do you see this? We have been called out of darkness to display our Father's character through Jesus Christ—the *seven eyes* and *seven radiations* of God that are moving through the earth in these last days. But if we disobey and disbelieve, we will stumble. It is time to come back to our Father's house and embrace our Father's ways.

~

God is in the process of rebuilding His church! And it will be accomplished the same way—through the orderly flow of the anointing.

~

You are a chosen race, a royal priesthood, a dedicated nation, [God's] own purchased, special people.

—1 PETER 2:9

89

The Seven Spirits of God

he seven spirits in Isaiah 11:1–3 describe the character attributes of our Father. These supernatural characteristics are being given to every son and daughter of the kingdom that will hear His voice and obey.

The *Spirit of the Lord* reflects the authority of God as "the existing One," Lord and Master of the earth. As you submit to Christ's authority, you will walk in consistent authority over the enemy.

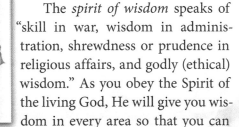

The perfecting work of God in His saints has intensified in this spiritual season.

The *spirit of wisdom* speaks of "skill in war, wisdom in administration, shrewdness or prudence in religious affairs, and godly (ethical) wisdom." As you obey the Spirit of the living God, He will give you wisdom in every area so that you can war effectively in this final hour.

The *spirit of understanding* adds perfected insight, natural and spiritual, to the wisdom of the Lord to help you walk securely. Through the *spirit of counsel*, God will advise you.

Through the *spirit of might*, God will give you strength to be equal to any task that is before you.

The *spirit of knowledge* adds perception and practical skill to wisdom and understanding. He is going to sharpen both your perception and the skills to match, so that you can finish what He has called you to do.

The *spirit of the fear of the Lord* keeps everything in check. As a true son or daughter in this season, you will have great honor and respect for the Lord—and as a result, every other gift and ability will flow in and through you like a mighty river. We are in the season of the supernatural—the day of "natural strength" is over.

~

Too many people have been trying to operate in the things of the Spirit without the authority, wisdom, understanding, counsel, might, knowledge, and fear of the Lord!

~

And the Spirit of the Lord shall rest upon Him—the Spirit of wisdom and understanding, the Spirit of counsel and might, the Spirit of knowledge and of the reverential and obedient fear of the Lord—and shall make Him of quick understanding, and His delight shall be in the reverential and obedient fear of the Lord.

—ISAIAH 11:2–3

90

The Seven Lamps of God

$\mathcal{I}$n Zechariah 4:1–7, we discover the seven lamps of God. The church is being restored by the supernatural flow of the anointing! The lampstand with seven lamps is the same *golden lampstand* (menorah) that was in the original tabernacle. But on top of it was something that wasn't in the tabernacle—a bowl with an olive tree on either side and seven pipes running from it down to each lamp (candlestick). Oil was flowing continuously into the bowl from each olive tree, which then flowed through the pipes to the lamps.

> *Your total ability to either follow or lead will be the result of spiritual union with our Father in heaven.*

A lampstand has one branch in the center (like a trunk) and six branches attached to the center (which represents the number of man). It was formed and beaten with pure gold...without wood or measurements. To me, this speaks that the lampstand can only hold the illumination of the Spirit of the Lord supernaturally. Human effort and earthly wisdom can't operate in this realm. Praise be to

God, it also means there are unlimited resources we receive from the *seven eyes* and *seven spirits* of God—if we stay in spiritual alignment.

The oil of the anointing is flowing directly from the Father through Jesus Christ by the power of the Holy Spirit to strengthen His church. Do you see why you must get in the place God has for you (in the church) and submit yourself to divine authority? This is a solemn word, and the consequences—good or bad—will be eternal.

So hear me: your power or ability as a son or daughter to submit to your spiritual parents is going to be possible only through the Holy Spirit. And if you are a spiritual parent, you will only be able to lead by the power of the Holy Ghost! The flesh will profit nothing. The arm of the flesh will fail in this hour. Your total ability to either follow or lead will be the result of spiritual union with our Father in heaven.

~

The oil of the anointing is flowing directly from the Father through Jesus Christ by the power of the Holy Spirit to strengthen His church.

~

As to the hidden meaning (the mystery) of…the seven lampstands of gold…the seven lampstands are the seven churches.

—REVELATION 1:20

91

The *Urim* and the *Thummim*

Under the Old Covenant, the high priest wore a breastplate that contained twelve stones—one for each tribe of Israel. Inside of the breastplate was a piece of parchment containing the ineffable name of God. Through this parchment, *Urim* (light) and *Thummim* (completeness) caused individual letters of the tribal names on the breastplate to light up. If read in the right order, he received the "complete and true answer" to the prayers for the nation of Israel.[*]

> You must submit to Jesus Christ through the ministry of the Holy Spirit, or life will not flow through you to others.

What does this mean today? I believe that through a "supernatural" release of *urim* and *thummim*, true sons and daughters will be able to see what God has placed in the "bosoms" of their spiritual parents. I also believe God will use these same spiritual elements to illuminate the hearts of leaders and give insight for those under their care. Human

---

[*]Rabbi Nosson Scherman, *The Chumash*, The Artscroll Series/Stone Edition (Brooklyn, NY: Mesorah Publications, Ltd., 1998, 2000), 47.

patterns and formulas will no longer work; only the pattern of the Lord will prosper.

To continually tap into this supernatural oil, our lives will have to remain pure before the Lord. Otherwise, spiritual life will cease. Under the Old Covenant, if a priest tried to serve without consecrating first, he would die just trying to step foot into the holy place. By and large, leadership isn't pure enough to possess the *urim* and *thummim* in the breastplate, which represents righteousness (Eph. 6:14). Where righteousness is in question, there can be no life.

The conditions of our society are so extreme that leaders can no longer lead by intellect. We have to be led by the Spirit. We must possess the *seven eyes* and *seven spirits* of God by way of the *seven lamps*. If you are a leader, you must submit to Jesus Christ through the ministry of the Holy Spirit, or life will not flow through you to others.

∼

Where righteousness is in question, there can be no life.

∼

Stand therefore [hold your ground], having tightened the belt of truth around your loins and having put on the breastplate of integrity and of moral rectitude and right standing with God.

—EPHESIANS 6:14

92

The Two Olive Trees

The two olive trees are also very prophetic. Many scholars believe the olive trees represent the kingly and priestly offices of Israel. This was fulfilled in Zechariah's day because Zerubbabel was a civil leader, and Joshua was the high priest. As "adopted" sons and daughters, we are kings and priests unto God in the supernatural realm (1 Pet. 2:9).

Only those who are in proper spiritual alignment will be divinely used in this final hour.

There is another meaning of the olive trees that I believe is significant, because it talks about events that take place during the tribulation period before Christ returns. Revelation 11:3–5 says, "And I will grant the power of prophecy to My two witnesses for 1,260 (42 months; three and one-half years), dressed in sackcloth. *These [witnesses] are the two olive trees and the two lampstands which stand before the Lord of the earth.* And if anyone attempts to injure them, fire pours from their mouth and consumes their enemies; if anyone should attempt to harm them, thus he is doomed to be slain" (emphasis added).

These two witnesses were given supernatural authority in the heavenly and earthly realms to bind, loose, and speak the word of the Lord. Power is building in the body of Christ toward the day when these two witnesses will declare the word of the Lord according to the *seven eyes* and *seven spirits*. Not long after, the kingdoms of this earth will become the kingdom of our God and His Christ! (See Revelation 11:15.)

Is your spirit picking up where the body of Christ is in God's prophetic plan? I sincerely hope so—because only those who are in proper spiritual alignment according to the orderly flow of the anointing will be divinely used in this final hour. Those who aren't will miss the mark.

~

As "adopted" sons and daughters, we are kings and priests unto God in the supernatural realm.

~

To Him Who ever loves us and has once [for all] loosed and freed us from our sins by His own blood, and formed us into a kingdom (a royal race), priests to His God and Father—to Him be the glory and the power and the majesty and the dominion throughout the ages and forever and ever.

—Revelation 1:5–6

93

Submission Breaks the Yoke of the Enemy

*T*he oil of the anointing is breaking every yoke of bondage—and according to the *seven lamps*, it isn't ever going to stop. But hear me. The Spirit of the Lord will only break yokes for those who have submitted themselves according to His pattern. You must be a true son or daughter of the kingdom, not a spiritual *lone ranger* with a personal agenda. If you have removed yourself from God's covering through a divinely appointed spiritual father or mother, you have exposed yourself to the enemy.

The latter glory of the church will be greater than the former!

But for true sons and daughters of the kingdom, Haggai 2:6–9 gives this promise: "Yet once more, in a little while, I will shake and make tremble the [starry] heavens, the earth, the sea, and the dry land; and I will shake all nations and the desire and the precious things of all nations shall come in, and I will fill this house with splendor, says the Lord of hosts. The silver is Mine and the gold is Mine, says the Lord of hosts. The latter glory of this house [with its successor, to which Jesus came] shall be greater than the former, says the Lord of hosts; and in this place will I give peace and prosperity, says the Lord of hosts."

Do you see God's promise? The *latter glory* of the church will be greater than the former! We are in the greatest supernatural season that has ever been known to man. But it's *by the Spirit*, not by human knowledge, wisdom, gifts, or talents. This means the days of spiritual showboating, politicking, name-dropping, and the like are screeching to a halt. Now more than ever, we should be rejoicing in the fact that we are sons and daughters of the gospel.

~

The Spirit of the Lord will only break yokes for those who have submitted themselves according to His pattern.

~

The latter glory of this house [with its successor, to which Jesus came] shall be greater than the former, says the Lord of hosts; and in this place will I give peace and prosperity, says the Lord of hosts.

—HAGGAI 2:9

94

Our True Inheritance

Today's church is so much like the prodigal son—we have taken the physical portion of our inheritance and left our father's house to waste it on our own desires. Our *true inheritance*—the supernatural character of our Father through Jesus Christ and the ministry of the Holy Spirit—is waiting to be restored to us *in the house of our spiritual father.*

God is shaking things today just as He was in Zerubbabel's time. And He is calling every member of the body of Christ to sonship through the same royal line. God has chosen us; we are that prodigal son. By the power of the Holy Spirit, He has made His true sons and daughters to be a "signet ring" in this hour.

The spirit of "fathers" is returning to the earth as leaders are turning to our heavenly Father.

This means we must reflect our heavenly Father's "image and likeness" to the world—His divine character. When people see God's people, they should see Jesus.

We are living in the days of Malachi 4:6: "And he shall turn and reconcile the hearts of the [estranged] fathers to the [ungodly] children, and the hearts of the [rebellious] children to [the piety of] their fathers [a reconciliation produced by repentance of the ungodly], lest I come and smite the land with a curse and a ban of utter destruction."

The spirit of "fathers" is returning to the earth as leaders are turning to our heavenly Father. As this happens, the orderly flow of the anointing is rising up and breaking every yoke of bondage. No weapon formed against God's church will prosper! God is restoring the true pattern of worship so His people will become a bride, *spotless* and *without blemish*, prepared for Christ's return.

⁓

Our true inheritance—the supernatural character of our Father through Jesus Christ and the ministry of the Holy Spirit—is waiting to be restored to us in the house of our spiritual father.

⁓

And he shall turn and reconcile the hearts of the [estranged] fathers to the [ungodly] children, and the hearts of the [rebellious] children to [the piety of] their fathers [a reconciliation produced by repentance of the ungodly], lest I come and smite the land with a curse and a ban of utter destruction.

—MALACHI 4:6

Section Fifteen

It's Time to Rebuild

95

The Enemy's Days Are Numbered!

*L*ike Israel in Zerubbabel's day, as we receive our true inheritance we can continue the mighty work of rebuilding the church. This work of rebuilding can be better understood by looking at the example of Ezra, who was called by God to rebuild the temple in Jerusalem after the Babylonian captivity of the children of Israel. (See Ezra 1:1–4.)

As we look at Ezra, it is important to note that Ezra wasn't the high priest—that was Joshua's role. But God used Ezra mightily in the rebuilding. He had great favor with the dignitaries that ruled over Israel. Cyrus was one of those kings. Under King Cyrus, Persia and its ally (Media) conquered the Babylonians nearly seventy years after they had taken Israel into captivity.

A day of reckoning is coming.

Babylon is where the goddess Ashtaroth came into being. I don't think it's a coincidence that God's people were set free by Cyrus, a Gentile king who had taken authority over Israel's ancient enemy! What makes this even more powerful is the fact that on the same night Belshazzar (Nebuchadnezzar's son) had a big "Babylonian" feast, bringing out the sacred vessels of Israel's temple to drink wine, God snatched the kingdom out of his hands. (See Daniel 5.)

Right in the middle of their party, God wrote Babylon's death sentence on the wall (Dan. 5:5). Daniel interpreted the inscription, and that night Belshazzar was killed. The kingdom of Babylonia fell to the Medes and Persians.

That's when God stirred up Cyrus' spirit. Cyrus decreed for the Israelites to rebuild the temple in Jerusalem—nearly *seventy years* after they had been taken captive in Babylon.

If we, God's people, will walk in our true inheritance according to the *seven eyes*, *seven spirits*, and *seven lamps* . . . Jezebel cannot usurp our God-given authority! Jesus has already freed us from the curse of this deceptive spirit.

~

The enemy's days are numbered.

~

This is the interpretation of the matter: MENE, God has numbered the days of your kingship and brought them to an end; TEKEL, You are weighed in the balances and are found wanting; PERES, Your kingdom and your kingship are divided and given to the Medes and Persians.

—DANIEL 5:26–28

96

True Praise Builds the Church

The church, under the prophetic anointing of Cyrus, is beginning to be rebuilt. Everything the enemy has stolen must be returned—because we have a great task to complete for our Father. The glory of the latter house will be greater than the former!

Even in Cyrus's day, Babylon came down and the leaders rose up. (See Ezra 1:3–7.) When it was time to rebuild the temple, God started the process by the power of His Spirit, much as He is doing today. He worked through the "spiritual fathers" He had appointed in the earth.

Everyone must serve according to the "measure of faith" God has given them.

Ezra 3:2–3 shows us the pattern for God's restoration. "They built the altar of the God of Israel to offer burnt offerings upon it, as it is written in the instructions of Moses the man of God. And they set the altar [in its place] upon its base, for fear was upon them because of the peoples of the countries; and they offered burnt offerings on it to the Lord morning and evening."

True worship was restored according the pattern of the tabernacle that God had originally revealed to Moses. After true worship was restored, "the fear of the Lord" came upon the people—and that started releasing everything else.

The priestly service came into order at the same time the temple's foundation was being laid. (See Ezra 3:8–11.) This couldn't have been a coincidence—it was divine destiny! And that's when true praise went up to God—according to the order of King David, a "father" of Israel and a *true son* of the kingdom. This is why spiritual alignment must be reestablished. When we worship God according to His pattern, He builds the church—and the gates of hell cannot prevail against it.

A great shaking is taking place in the body of Christ, and this process is of the Lord! Everyone must serve according to the "measure of faith" God has given them—and this will restore us to God's pattern. The Spirit of the Lord is rebuilding His church!

~

True worship is built on the foundation of godly character.

~

And all the people shouted with a great shout when they praised the Lord, because the foundation of the house of the Lord was laid!

—Ezra 3:11

97

Beware of the Enemy's Sabotage

*T*he devil always tries to sabotage God's plan. He did in the days of Ezra's rebuilding, and he will in this day. (See Ezra 4:1–5). Israel had been delivered from Babylon, so the "chameleon" spirit of Jezebel transformed…and came back through the Samaritans. The enemy will do anything to stop the work of God, including coming to you as an "angel of light." He can only succeed by coming where you are and making you give up what is rightfully yours.

The church cannot be hindered if we stay in spiritual alignment.

Israel's fathers saw right through it. They told the Samaritans, "You don't have anything to do with this…" Then the warfare intensified. The enemy hired professional "counselors" and sent them into Israel to frustrate the work of God. Eventually, Israel's enemies wore God's people down, and they stopped building.

How could this have happened? Between verses 6 and 9 in the fourth chapter, the enemy kept building a stronghold. When Ashtaroth perceives a threat in the spirit realm, the spirit of Jezebel will always rise up and try to match your strength. In the end, more than eleven enemy nations joined together and wrote a letter of complaint against Israel to Artaxerxes (king of Persia during that time).

The Israelites had replied with these words: "We are servants of the God of heaven and earth, rebuilding the house which was erected and finished many years ago by a great king of Israel" (Ezra 5:11).

The church cannot be hindered if we stay in spiritual alignment! Notice this: when the people of God drop our names and titles, we take on our Father's identity. When a man's ways please the Lord, even his enemies will be at peace with him (Prov. 16:7). Not only did King Darius honor Cyrus's decree to strongly establish the foundations of the church, but he also decreed that everything Israel needed for the sacrifices would be provided…*daily without fail.* Prosperity hits your life when you become a servant.

~

When the people of God drop our names and titles, we take on our Father's identity.

~

We are servants of the God of heaven and earth, rebuilding the house which was erected and finished many years ago by a great king of Israel.

—Ezra 5:11

98

The Seven Attributes of True Worship

*E*ach of the seven sacrificial elements that Darius restored to Israel gives a powerful revelation of how the Father's character operates in His sons and daughters.

In the Old Testament tabernacle, a *young bull* was sacrificed in the sin offering. As a true son or daughter you always seek to give your best to God. Two *rams* were also part of the sacrifice: one as a burnt offering and sweet savor unto the Lord, and one for consecration. You must willingly separate yourself to pray and make intercession for others. *Two lambs* were sacrificed daily: one in the morning and one in the evening, and you willingly take up the cross and follow the Lord—morning, noon, and night.

As a son or daughter of the gospel, the process of "pressing" in your life has yielded the peaceable fruit of righteousness.

Wheat, salt, wine, and oil generally speak of the goodness of the Lord, His mercy, joy, and refreshing. *Wheat* represents provision and blessing. *Salt* was rubbed onto the meat for every sacrifice, just as you truly are "the salt of the earth" as God's child.

Both *wine* and *oil* go through a process of pressing. As a son or daughter of the gospel, the process of "pressing" in your life has yielded the peaceable fruit of righteousness.

The *oil* represents the anointing of the Holy Spirit and was used to anoint the tabernacle—all the tabernacle elements as well as Aaron and his sons. The anointing will be evident as you serve. The Holy Spirit prepares and empowers you for every task.

These "sacrificial elements" are the fourth group of seven. *Four* speaks of the *supernatural manifestation* of God. Remember, all seven elements were given to Israel's leaders (the servants of God in Ezra 5:11) through a leader (King Darius). You have to stay in spiritual alignment to receive the inheritance of the Lord.

~

These seven sacrificial elements are a powerful confirmation that you have received your true inheritance.

~

Except the Lord builds the house, they labor in vain who build it; except the Lord keeps the city, the watchman wakes but in vain.

—Psalm 127:1

99

The House of the Lord Will Be Completed

*A*s leaders submit to God (the *seven eyes*), authority, understanding, wisdom, counsel, might, knowledge, and the fear of the Lord (the *seven spirits*) will build the church from the ground up. And as long as we stay under the flow of the Spirit by way of the *seven lamps*, God's people will not be hindered—the church will be restored, just as it was in Ezra's day!

Spiritual alignment is being restored to the church. That's why the seven lamps are overflowing with oil in this final hour. That's why things are shaking in the realm of the Spirit! The kingdoms of the earth must become the kingdoms of our God and His Christ. *We are in transition.* Hear me. Don't resist the workings of God, because He gave us a "Son" so that we could become sons and daughters.

It is time for the church to stop running from the enemy—he has already been defeated!

We see the completion of God's pattern for restoration in Ezra 6:18–22. The priests purified themselves, and *then* the

Israelites separated themselves to seek the Lord. The anointing flowed through proper spiritual alignment, and true worship was birthed in God's people, evidenced because they received *an inheritance*, not just a physical portion. God will give great favor and strengthen our hands to rebuild His church, but we must be obedient. Leaders must obey the voice of the Father, and sons and daughters must honor leadership.

Remember, a mighty inheritance awaits you in your Father's house: *seven eyes, seven spirits, seven lamps*, and *seven sacrificial elements*—a supernatural portion that can't be shaken.

~

Return to spiritual alignment, and the Holy Spirit will bring down every enemy of the cross in your life.

~

For to us a Child is born, to us a Son is given; and the government shall be upon His shoulder, and His name shall be called Wonderful Counselor, Mighty God, Everlasting Father [of Eternity], Prince of Peace. Of the increase of His government and of peace there shall be no end, upon the throne of David and over his kingdom, to establish it and to uphold it with justice and with righteousness from the [latter] time forth, even forevermore.

—Isaiah 9:6–7

100

Closing Letter—My Spiritual Inheritance

*I*n this final hour, the hearts of the fathers are being restored to their children, and true sons and daughters of the gospel are being birthed according to Malachi 4:6. This process of restoration is the key to unlocking our spiritual inheritance. It is also why a strong attack has been launched by the enemy against proper spiritual alignment in the body of Christ and the local church.

Delivering this word wasn't easy. It has weighed heavily in my spirit, so I expect it will continue to do the same in yours…because possessing your spiritual inheritance is definitely a weighty matter. It is far more important than merely receiving material blessings; it is about returning to our heavenly Father's house and taking on the attributes of His character. In this prophetic season, it will be a sure defense against the enemy's devices.

If you are looking for your spiritual parents, let me give you a word of hope. Psalm 68:5 tells us that our God is "a father of the fatherless, and a judge of the widows" (KJV). Even if you don't have a spiritual father at this moment, God still cares for you. He is willing and able to cover and guide you to your spiritual home.

Now, listen closely. This is the time you must begin to follow the divine instructions of your heavenly Father as He prepares you to walk in obedience to your spiritual father. It's important that you keep your spirit purified, as David did, to hear His every instruction. God will send you a spiritual father and mother on earth for the areas in the natural where you need to be led. When the student is ready, the teacher will show up.

I urge you to take every issue God has brought to the surface as you were following this devotional study to Him in prayer. Now you know the dangers of a corrupt spiritual lineage—and you know the blessings of a godly one. Decide today to be a son or daughter of the kingdom, obedient to the voice of your heavenly Father, and submitted to those He has given to you as a spiritual covering here on earth.

There is always hope when you put your trust in Jesus. He's the real authority. No devil can stop Him from leading you into your divine destiny—*but you can.* He has given you the power to choose. I beseech you today by the mercies of God to present yourself to Jesus as a living sacrifice and choose to obey His Word.

SUBMITTED TO HIS WORD,
JUANITA BYNUM

Strang Communications, the publisher of both Charisma House and _Charisma_ magazine, wants to give you 3 FREE ISSUES of our award-winning magazine.

Since its inception in 1975, _Charisma_ magazine has helped thousands of Christians stay connected with what God is doing worldwide.

Within its pages you will discover in-depth reports and the latest news from a Christian perspective, biblical health tips, global events in the body of Christ, personality profiles, and so much more. Join the family of _Charisma_ readers who enjoy feeding their spirit each month with miracle-filled testimonies and inspiring articles that bring clarity, provoke prayer, and demand answers.

To claim your **3 free issues** of _Charisma,_ send your name and address to: Charisma 3 Free Issue Offer, 600 Rinehart Road, Lake Mary, FL 32746. Or you may call 1-800-829-3346 and ask for Offer # 93FREE. This offer is only valid in the USA.

---

www.charismamag.com